Politics
of
Arlington, Texas

An Era of Continuity and Growth

by

Allan Saxe

EAKIN PRESS ✏ Fort Worth, Texas
www.EakinPress.com

All proceeds accruing to the author of this book will be donated to the Arlington Public Library Foundation and the Arlington Historical Association.

Copyright © 2001
By Allan Saxe
Published By Eakin Press
An Imprint of Wild Horse Media Group
P.O. Box 331779
Fort Worth, Texas 76163
1-817-344-7036
www.EakinPress.com
ALL RIGHTS RESERVED
1 2 3 4 5 6 7 8 9
ISBN-10: 1-57168-542-1
ISBN-13: 978-1-571685-42-1

Library of Congress Cataloging-in-Publication Data

Saxe, Allan A.
    Politics of Arlington : an era of continuity and growth / Allan Saxe.--1st ed.
       p.   cm.
    Includes index.
    ISBN 1-57168-542-1
    1. Arlington (Tex.)--Politics and government--20th century. 2. Politicians--Texas--Arlington--History--20th century. 3. Politicians--Texas--Arlington--Biography. I. Title.

F394.A74 S29 2001
976.4'531--dc21
                                              2001040530

Contents

Acknowledgments v
Introduction vii

One: Political Setting and Structure 1
Two: The Atmosphere 15
Three: The Vandergriff Years........................ 20
    Arlington Leaders Forge Elite Governance 24
    The Emergence of Mayoral Authority 28
Four: Post Vandergriff: Continuity and Growth
with Three Mayors.................................. 44
Five: Winners, Losers, Movers, Shakers:
Shaping City Politics................................ 71
    Betty and Nile Fischer 71
    Barton Thompson vs. Martha Walker and
        Ralph Shelton vs. Paul Yarbrough................ 80
    Sam Hamlett 88
    Ken Groves...................................... 92
    Jim Norwood 95
    Richard (Dick) Malec............................. 99
    George Hawkes 101
    Dr. R.G. "Wick" Alexander 104
    James Martin................................... 107

Dottie Lynn 109
Kelly Jones 112
Roger "Rocky" Walton 115
Kay Taebel 117
Tom Cravens 119
The City Managers 122
A New Leader Emerges: Elzie Odom 129

Six: Mavericks, Naysayers, and Watchdogs:
The Conscience of a Community 132
    Joyce Morgan 133
    Harry Robinson 134
    Lico Reyes 135
    Roy George "Skippy" Brown III 137
    Bill Eastland 139
    Kathy Howe 140

Conclusion
    The Political Establishment in Decline 145

Appendix A   Interviews 149
Appendix B   Arlington Mayors 151
Appendix C   Arlington Mayors from 1884 to 2000 153
Appendix D   City Council, October 1919 to May 2000 . . . 155
Appendix E   30 Years of City Elections,
Arlington, Texas 159
Appendix F   Arlington Mayors & Commissioners,
1921-1956 161
Appendix G   Arlington Elected Officials &
Election Results, 1957-2000 164
Appendix H   Arlington City Attorneys 173
Notes 174
Index 181

Acknowledgments

The author is indebted to all persons interviewed. Their years of experiences and public service needed to be documented. Hopefully, this book will, in part, bring their contributions and history to public view.

Thanks to the *Fort Worth Star-Telegram* photograph collection in the University of Texas at Arlington Special Collections Archive, and to the assistance of Donita Maligi. Allowing the use of their photographs in this work has been invaluable.

Thanks to the City Secretary's Office of the City of Arlington. The help and assistance of their staff in obtaining relevant documents were essential to this book.

Thanks to Ruthie Brock, reference librarian in the University of Texas at Arlington Libraries. Her attention to detail was of great importance. Without her motivation the book never would have been started or completed.

Finally, thanks to all who have contributed to the political scene in Arlington during the era studied. Whether they were winners or losers, observers or active participants, they have kept the democratic light burning brightly.

Introduction

This is a chronicle of the politics, policies, and personalities of the city council of Arlington, Texas, from the post-World War II era to early 1997. Even though there has been some overlapping between school and city politics, this study will pivot primarily on the city council. The history and politics of the Arlington Independent School District is worthy of study, but should be examined in a separate work.

This work will attempt to define and describe those public and private persons who influenced the politics of the city. The Arlington city council and the office of mayor will be explored in regard to the elections which filled these posts, the decisions made, the people who made the decisions, and the purpose behind their actions.

In writing this study, primary sources were extensively utilized. Personal interviews with many of the personalities who molded city politics, newspaper articles, and documents from the city secretary's office were used. Academic texts that examine local politics on a broader scale were used for comparative purposes in analyzing Arlington's political background.

Though this study is primarily a chronicle, it is also an interpretation of what happened, why it happened, and who benefited or lost. The structure and power centers of the city's politics will be explored. This study will pivot on the city council, the office of mayor, and other important personalities, both public and private, who have had an impact on the direction of the city. It is a case study of the politics of a booming mid-size American city.

Arlington's course was mostly determined and directed by high-level elected and appointed officials. But as in all political entities, some non-elected people had important backstage roles. Their roles and influence will be covered as well.

An attempt will be made not only to identify and understand the decision-makers in the Arlington community, but to present the main political events and episodes as well.

It must be emphasized that this is not a historical chronicle. The primary theme is politics and power. Historical events will be identified only to highlight the political process as it developed.

This study was directed and compiled principally by utilizing primary information. This approach included, first and foremost, interviews conducted with those people identified as significant players in the political course of Arlington, Texas.

The interviewees were selected for their roles as elected or appointed city officials during the time period studied. Inclusion of others is based on mention by the press or civic activists or by recommendation from the general citizenry.

Secondary sources utilized were newspaper reports, records of the city secretary's office, and city council minutes and records. Comparison political studies of other communities will be mentioned when appropriate.

Additionally, the author of this study has been an ardent observer of city politics, a candidate for city council, and a columnist. Having run, unsuccessfully, in 1975 for a city council position, the author returned to being solely an interested observer whose participation in this writing was both an asset and a motivation.

What is the importance of a political study of Arlington, Texas? This largely unnoticed city has grown dramatically from being a small, homogeneous town nestled between Fort

Worth and Dallas, to a full-grown, mature, heterogeneous community competing for entertainment, sports, business organizations, quality of living, and population size.

The kind of governance Arlington had in various stages of development will be explored. How much of Arlington's growth was motivated by political leadership and how much by its location will be examined.

There are other United States cities that have experienced similar spectacular growth records. This study of the politics of Arlington, Texas, may be useful to students of comparable communities. Was Arlington, Texas, a unique community in its political architecture and style, or was it similar to others?

It is hoped that this work will be useful both to the academic and to the general public. Cities have always been taken for granted, especially when they work, but what they do to achieve success is critical. At the core of city life and duty are the effectiveness of various departments: sanitation, police, fire, and water, to name a few. Also essential to a city's success is how and where its citizens live and do business. This study of how politics has been interwoven with the civic life of Arlington, Texas, may be instructive.

Chapter One

Political Setting and Structure

At the close of World War II the city of Arlington, Texas, was a very small town. It was located midway between the two larger and widely recognized cities of Fort Worth and Dallas. Its land area was only a few square miles and its population was very small. The Arlington name derives from Robert E. Lee's home place in Virginia.

From its incorporation as a city on March 18, 1884, Arlington did not grow rapidly in land size or in population for the next six decades.

O.K. Carter, a longtime city resident, local historian, and editorial writer for the *Arlington Star-Telegram,* stated that at the time of its incorporation in 1884 "Arlington's land area was a half-mile square."[1] Its population in 1894 was 900 according to the city secretary's office. From that date until 1940 the population did not increase more than 1,500 from decade to decade. By the end of World War II the city's population and land area had increased slightly. In 1950, 7,692 people lived within a four-square-mile area.

In at least one way, the city's early history was not unlike other small southern communities. Records of the Arlington city secretary's office indicate that a chapter of the Ku Klux Klan,

"Knight of Honor, Arlington Lodge #3811," existed in the community for a few years early in the twentieth century.

However, it did have its unique qualities. It became known early on in two widely different areas. Arlington was of note to people out of the immediate area as a home for a horseracing track named Arlington Downs, which operated from 1928 to 1936.

In a different segment of community life, the city was the site of a college, originally named Arlington College, founded in 1895. The college developed through six name changes until its present status as a full-scale university now known as the University of Texas at Arlington (UTA). In large degree, the growth of UTA parallels the growth and development of the city.

Aside from the well-known General Motors plant, the Texas Rangers baseball club, and Six Flags, the city was home for many years to corporations doing nationwide business, among them Oil States Rubber, Martin Sprocket and Gear, Doskocil Manufacturing, Decision Analyst, Miller Business Systems, and National Semiconductor.

Arlington's unique location, close to and between Fort Worth and Dallas, made it a convenient stop for travelers between these two larger cities. Arlington became easy to identify to people in distant parts of Texas and in other states simply by describing its location between Dallas and Fort Worth.

But residents always felt that the city did not garner its share of recognition. In the late 1960s, the author remembers some Dallas residents remarking that Arlington was only "a junior college surrounded by used car lots." This reference was to the university and to the numerous used car lots located in its downtown area at the time. Another common reference labeled Arlington as being the dash between Dallas and Fort Worth.

Well into the last part of the twentieth century some civic leaders were still sensitive to any identification of Arlington as simply being midway between Dallas and Fort Worth. Corporate brochures of the North Texas region that identified only Fort Worth and Dallas as major cities in the area came in for correction.

When Arlington was mentioned as being a suburban

area, that description was not received well. Mayor Richard Greene set the record clear when he declared several times during his tenure of office, "Arlington is nobody's suburb."

Clearly, Arlington's political leadership from the end of World War II to the end of the century had one goal in mind. Arlington would be a major city. There would be those in the community who wished that Arlington would retain its small-town aura, but they would be mostly on the losing side.

The principal issue of growth would divide the political establishment from others in the community. Arlington would, if the political leaders had their way, no longer be an overlooked suburb.

At the end of World War II, as in earlier years, Arlington's city government was structured around a commission form of government. There were four commissioners and a mayor. All were elected at large. Each commissioner had responsibility for a specific portion of municipal operations. There was a Commissioner of Water, a Commissioner of Police and Fire, a Commissioner of Streets and Roads, and a Commissioner of Finance. The mayor was assigned general oversight responsibilities.[2]

The four commissioners and the mayor were elected for two-year terms of office that had no term limitations. They all could be re-elected, in alternating years, for as many terms as the electorate wished. The mayor and commissioners were paid ten dollars a month. Under the commission form of government in Arlington only white males traditionally were elected to the office of mayor and commissioner.

In the 1940s, under the commission form of government, "council meetings were closed to the public and could be called as often as the mayor and council members deemed necessary without public notice."[3]

At this time and until 1967 there was no state Open Meetings Act. The first Open Meetings Act was passed in 1967, then strengthened and amended in subsequent years. The first state Open Records Act was passed in 1973 and amended in 1993. It is clear that in its early stages the politics of Texas cities was more insulated from public scrutiny.

The commission form of government was commonly utilized in small- and medium-sized towns and cities throughout the state. Dallas, Texas, utilized early in its political history a commission city government. It was thought to be a useful form of political architecture for efficiency and money savings. Here, publicly elected commissioners would directly control and supervise fire, police, sanitation, and other municipal responsibilities. As cities grew, these functions would be performed by paid professionals. This system would be implemented in Arlington at a later date.

In June 1949 the Arlington city charter was amended to hire a city manager. City leaders understood that even though the municipality was quite small the demands and functions of a city poised to grow in population and size demanded more professional oversight.

The city manager would now be responsible for hiring department heads and overseeing the daily operations of city government.

In January 1950 the city hired its first city manager, Albert Jones. His tenure would be very short, lasting only until August of the same year. The commissioners then hired O.B. Odell, who in his five-year tenure saw Arlington through its first rapid population-growth period.

The city still maintained its commission form of government after the formal addition of the city manager. It could be characterized from 1949 to 1960 as a "commissioner-manager" form of city government.

In 1960, through another city charter amendment process, the government would alter itself yet again. This process formally changed the name from commissioner member to council member. This action would fit nicely with the growing professionalism in the management of Arlington's municipal government.

Arlington now had all the trappings of a council-manager form of government. At the same time as the name change to council member, the city charter was amended to expand the city council. The city council-city manager form of government would be kept in place for the rest of the twentieth century.

The expansion in council members in 1960 from four to

Political Setting and Structure 5

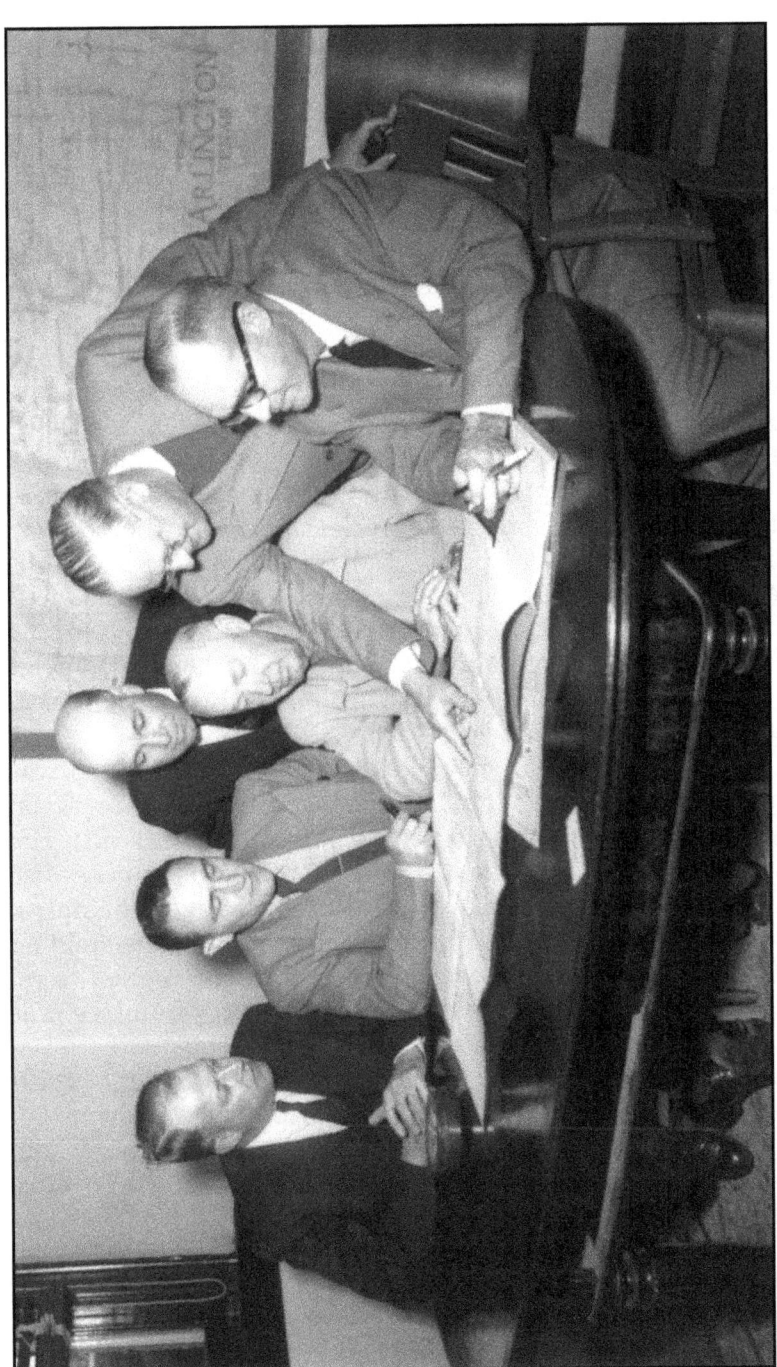

Arlington City Commissioners (8 January 1950).
—*Fort Worth Star-Telegram* Photograph Collection, Special Collections Division, The University of Texas at Arlington Libraries

six members plus the mayor was also in response to a dramatic rise in population. In 1960 the population had increased sixfold to 44,775 from its 1950 total of 7,692.[4] All council members and the mayor were elected at large, meaning each represented the entire city and was elected by the entire city electorate.

Through the mid-1960s, council votes were recorded orally as "ayes or nays." Electronic voting was added later. The discussions of the council were electronically recorded. Council meetings were held in a small municipal building at the corner of Abram and Pecan until moving on August 9, 1981, to a much larger building and council chambers at Abram and Center Streets.

For election purposes members of the city council were identified as representing a numerical place on the council. Council members would be elected representing Place One, Place Two, and so on, on an alternate two-year election cycle. If no candidate had a majority vote in the general election, the candidate with a simple plurality would be declared the winner. There were no provisions in the charter for a run-off election until the mid-1970s.

In 1980 through a city charter revision the council was expanded to a total of eight seats in addition to the mayor. Also, the mayor was now to be paid $250 a month with the council members receiving $200 a month. The mayor also would be given a vote similar to that of any council member.

Prior to this charter revision election, which was held on April 5, 1980, a committee was appointed by the council to review the city charter. The appointed review committee was composed of members from various city interests.

Representatives from organized labor, banking, education, politics, and civic life were appointed. The chairman of the charter review committee was former mayor Tom Vandergriff, who had voluntarily vacated the mayor's office three years earlier.

Tom Cravens, a member of a longtime banking family, and Gary Bruner were also members of the charter review committee. Bruner was a newcomer to Arlington whose work was in financial services. He later would become a council member and eventually mount a losing race for mayor. Other charter review members were: Dr. R.G. "Wick" Alexander, a former city council member and orthodontist; Bernadette Henz, a prominent church worker and civic leader; Bill Bennet, a member of organized labor; Allan Saxe of the education community; and Herman Veselka, a former city manager.

The review committee spent several months debating with one another, listening to citizen input, and eventually submitting proposals to the council. There were many lively discussions involving city politics. The issue of how council members ought to be elected, whether from single districts or the at-large system, was always prominent.

The review committee did take a vote on a mixed single member district-at-large plan. However, the proposal did not win a majority vote and thus was not submitted to the council for possible voter approval. More than a decade would pass before the council would submit such a proposal to the voters for charter revision. On November 2, 1993, the voters approved single-member districts. (See Table 1.1.)

In 1994, after many years of debate and controversy, the city held its first election under a mixed single-member district and at-large plan. A charter amendment, passed on November 2, 1993, now provided for five council seats to be elected from specific geographical areas (single districts) while three council positions in addition to the mayoral office would continue to be elected from the entire city (at-large).

From the mid-1970s and through the following decade, Arlington and many other communities would struggle with and debate over representation. Specifically, they contended with whether single-member or at-large representation best served the city. This debate and its eventual compromise resolution will be taken up in subsequent portions of this study. But it should be noted that the political establishment did at first perceive single-member representation as the single most serious challenge to their power.[5]

The city, during the time span covered, had no financial disclosure for elected officials. The state penal code pertains to serious ethical offenses such as gifts and misuse of government resources. The city code addressed matters of compen-

CITY OF ARLINGTON SINGLE MEMBER DISTRICT ELECTION NOVEMBER 2, 1993			
PRECINCTS	TOTAL VOTES	YES	NO
ATHERTON	678	474	175
BAILEY	834	277	511
BEBENSEE	688	426	214
BERRY	655	442	172
BLANTON	530	294	198
BOLES	710	332	323
COA/PARKS & REC	346	187	144
COREY	615	260	321
DITTO	695	279	377
DUFF	797	272	473
ELLIS	694	374	265
FITZGERALD	485	318	144
GUNN	768	329	399
MILLER	756	353	347
MORTON	625	347	227
POPE	813	345	420
SHACKELFORD	587	202	349
SHERROD	934	411	471
SOUTH DAVIS	432	193	218
THORNTON	446	313	108
WIMBISH	631	290	310
WOOD	770	297	423
YOUNG	998	417	531
EARLY	3,035	1,600	1,358
TOTALS	18,522	9,032	8,478

Table 1.1
Single Member District Election, 2 November 1993
City Secretary's Office, Arlington, Texas

sation for support of issues and promises of future employment from those having an interest in city council decisions. Council members recuse themselves from voting if there is a direct conflict of interest or impropriety.

All city elections in Arlington are held on a non-partisan basis. This means that there are no party primaries for city elections and no political party labels for council members and the mayor. This did not mean that partisan politics did not play a role in city politics, only that there was no partisan ballot identification.

The political party identification of various mayors and council members and their opponents was frequently known and acknowledged. Some city politicians at times openly supported partisan candidates and issues at play in county, state, and even national campaigns.

Partisanship did play a role in some city elections, but not a very visible one. Political party activists at times did make their preferences known. However, the non-partisanship of municipal politics still was the controlling factor.[6]

Until the early 1980s, the mayor had no vote in council meetings. Prior to this time, he was able to cast a vote to break tie votes. The mayor was given a vote during the mayoral tenure of S.J. Stovall.

Interestingly, the absence of a mayoral vote until the 1980s may have given early mayors more power. The mayor could simply deflect citizen pressure on various topics by stating that he did not have a vote. But behind the scenes the mayor could still have considerable leverage and power. "What a deal," stated Jewell Fox, a longtime Tarrant County political activist and observer. "The mayor did not have to commit himself to a yes or no vote, but could still act powerfully behind the scenes. This was a good way to keep your popularity while still getting things done your way."[7]

Until the early 1970s, there were no meaningful state laws dealing with open records or open meetings. For most of its early history the city council could, as a group of two or more members, gather informally at social events or other occasions and discuss city business, if they so wished. This type of gathering would never be allowed under present state laws without prior public notice.

The city of Arlington, Texas, now had under its new council-manager form of government a system categorized in political science texts as a "weak-mayor" council-manager form of government. The mayor formally had no veto power, could not submit a separate budget, could not make appointments without council consent, and had no authority over the day-to-day operations of the city.

However, this study will attempt to show that Arlington operated for many years under a weak mayor system in name only. Some Arlington mayors, as will be shown, were in reality very strong and powerful politically. This was due in part to their leadership personalities and a consensus they were able to form with community leaders.

The council-manager form of government operates in the following ways. The city council and the mayor select the city manager. The city manager is responsible to the council and the council can both hire and fire the occupant of this office. The city council makes policy while the city manager implements it.

In Arlington the only other high city offices directly responsible to the council and mayor by appointment are those of municipal judge and city attorney. In some council-manager systems municipal judges are elected, not appointed. Transferring the office of municipal judge to an elected position has been discussed and debated in Arlington, but never changed to date.

The city manager is appointed by the city council and serves at their pleasure. The city manager is responsible for all other city employees (as shown in Figure 1.1.) Arlington has no civil service system.[8]

The city conforms to state and national regulations in its hiring, promotion, and termination policies. The city manager, responsible for the day-to-day operations of the city, can hire and fire department heads, submit budgets for council examination, and must be present at all formal council sessions.

The council and mayor are charged with making overall policy decisions allowed under state law. This includes zoning

Political Setting and Structure

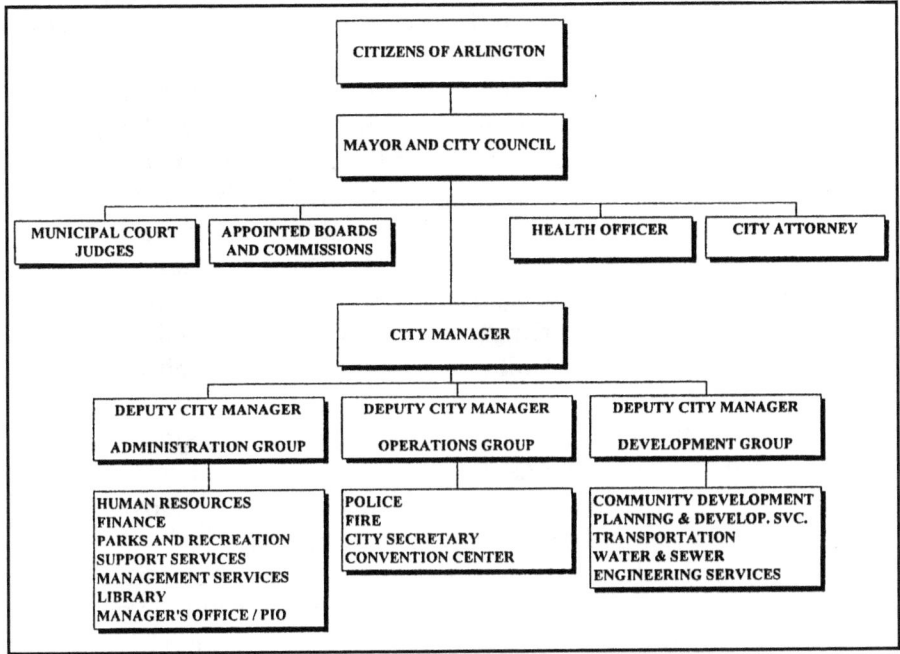

Figure 1.1

decisions, which are of paramount importance, and the drafting of city ordinances.

Their additional charges include: entering into contracts for purchase of goods and services; developing and overseeing master plans for the city's future; submitting proposals for elections; and considering citizen concerns on a wide variety of matters.

In Arlington some essential services were contracted out to private interests. Among the privatized areas were trash collection services, cable TV, ambulance services, and internal security at some public buildings.

Under the council-manager form of government the mayor and council are not allowed to interfere with the daily management and operations of the city.

This local government plan is utilized most frequently in medium-sized cities with populations from around 75,000 to 500,000. The city of Dallas, with over 1,000,000 people, is one of the largest cities in the nation with a council-manager form of government.

Many large cities in the country employ what is labeled a "strong-mayor" form of city government. The mayor, along with a partisan council, is most commonly elected under a political party label. Under this form of government, the mayor has wide powers of hiring and firing as well as extensive daily operating powers. New York City and Chicago are prime examples.

However, as of January 1997 Fort Worth and Dallas—both in close proximity to Arlington—utilized the council-manager form. As noted earlier, Dallas is one of the largest cities in the nation with a council-manager form of government.

Interestingly, early in 1997 there was discussion and debate about whether Dallas, because of its size and complexity, should invest the mayor with more power and move away from the council-manager form of government.[9]

Former Dallas mayor Steve Bartlett has said that Dallas needs major reform in the way its council and mayor govern. "The charter needs a wholesale revision and strengthening of the mayor's responsibility. We have a system (council-manager) that has worked well since the 1930s, but I think moving into the next century, the public has the right to hold their officials accountable for results."[10]

Longtime Dallas city council member Max Wells has said of the council-manager system, "The real difficulty of being mayor is that you have very limited power and yet the public tends to hold you responsible for success or failure . . . the council manager form of government (in Dallas, however) . . . has worked very well."[11]

At times Arlington has had the strength of a "strong mayor" city government without the formal categorization. This informal strong mayor system was superimposed on a more formal and institutionalized council-manager form. It could be said that the city had the best of both political worlds.

Complementing the council-manager form of government under which Arlington city government has functioned are a number of boards and commissions. They are established to give study and advice to the mayor and council on subjects under the purview of city government.

Among the most familiar are the Planning and Zoning Commission, Parks and Recreation Board, and Library Board. Others range in subject area from the Animal Shelter Advisory Committee to the Zoning Board of Adjustment.

All appointments are made by the mayor with the consent of the council, with the exception of the North Texas Higher Education Authority. The council appoints only part of its membership. Most of the boards and commissions make a report to the mayor and council where it is taken under advisement.

For most of the city's history, appointments to boards and commissions had no term limits attached. Most appointments were for two-year terms. However, some citizens served a long number of cumulative years due to repeated reappointments. This policy was later changed by the council to a slightly more restrictive policy to allow for turnover and hoped for better representation.

People are still named for two-year terms for most appointed boards and commissions. However, "It is intended that a person be eligible to serve up to three consecutive, full two year terms...." This action takes into account appointments to fill vacancies for unexpired terms. "After the completion of three consecutive two-year terms, a person is not eligible for appointment for one year."[12]

Persons who have served the maximum term on one designated board or commission may be appointed to a different one. However, persons cannot serve on two separate designated boards or commissions at the same time. Membership on these boards and commissions varies from five members on the Housing Authority Board, seven on the Hospital Authority, eleven on the Parks and Recreation Board, to eighteen on the Youth and Families Board.

During the period covered in this study only persons eligible to vote in city elections were eligible for appointment to boards and commissions. Early in the year 2000, a heated discussion arose whether to open appointment on some boards to those younger than eighteen years of age. Subsequently, a new policy allowing younger persons to serve on some boards was adopted.

For many years the most prestigious council-appointed board or commission has been the Planning and Zoning Commission. This nine-member board has traditionally been a stepping stone to the council. Perhaps the best example is that of Richard Greene, who was appointed to this board by Mayor Tom Vandergriff. Richard Greene was elected to the council later and subsequently to the office of mayor.

The city council then makes the final decision on all matters brought before it with the exception of a few very specialized appeal boards like the electrical, mechanical, and plumbing boards. Here, the board decisions are final and can only be reviewed again by appeal to a state district court.

Some municipalities by their charters allow boards and agencies to have substantially more authority than the purely advisory duties assigned to Arlington boards. Some city charters require a majority of council members to override board decisions.

Still these purely advisory boards and commissions in Arlington's governance offer the council important guidance and direction. Arlington politics, as this study will attempt to show, has pivoted primarily on establishing a consensus in the community.

The boards and commissions have been one of a number of political and social vehicles used to construct a consensus—a meeting of the minds, an agreement—on how to proceed on community agendas.

Appointments have been used to reward those in the community who have supported city officials and their agenda. In other cases, they may be used to defuse possible dissent. They have also been utilized, as exemplified by the Planning and Zoning Commission, to prepare people for higher city offices. This is a very natural process and not peculiar only to Arlington city politics.

Chapter Two

The Atmosphere

The year 1951 was crucial in Arlington politics. The city was still very small with a population hovering around 8,000 and with four square miles in land area.[1] The community was on the verge of major changes, but none were clearly visible yet.

Interestingly, the population of Grand Prairie, a city to the immediate east of Arlington, had a population in 1950 according to the United States Census double that of Arlington (14,594). During the next decade, Arlington's population would surpass that of Grand Prairie. In 1960 the United States Census reported Arlington, Texas, at 44,775. Grand Prairie had 30,386. Clearly, Arlington would be a much different city in 1960 than it was a decade earlier.

The city of Arlington in 1951 even had an airport located a bit north of the downtown area in a site later occupied by what became known as Town North Shopping Center. A famous mineral well in the downtown area was closed the same year. However, the citizens continued to get their drinking water from wells until a reservoir, Lake Arlington, was developed a few years later.

At the start of this pivotal year the mayor of the city was B.C. "Barney" Barnes, who had served in that position since

1947. B.C. Barnes was preceded in the mayor's office by W.F. Altman, who had been mayor since 1935. B.C. Barnes was a top administrator of business affairs for what was then known as Arlington State College—later to become the University of Texas at Arlington.

Prior to becoming mayor, he was a city commissioner from 1942 to 1944. His political views were consistent with much of the business community as it was then constituted. There were no major issues dividing him from the other decision-makers in town.

At least two local newspapers operated in the community during the period studied. Early on, one was the *Arlington Journal* and the other, *The Arlington Citizen*. They were to merge in 1957 into the *Arlington Citizen-Journal*.

Competition came from the *Arlington News-Texan*. Then another newspaper, the *Arlington Daily News,* owned by the Belo Corporation, operated for a time in the community as well. It covered Arlington's civic and political life, but never reached the influence of the *Citizen-Journal*.

The *Citizen-Journal*, under the leadership of George Hawkes, became an influential part of the civic and political life of Arlington. It was distributed to its loyal readers for a time by mail and was referred to affectionately as the "C-J."

In the early to mid-1970s, the *Arlington Daily News* did for a brief time assume a significantly different role from that of the dominant *Citizen-Journal*. This was especially true under the editorship of Les Blaser. It took a less "civic-boosterish" attitude than that of the *Citizen-Journal*.

Les Blaser, the editor of the *Arlington Daily News* who presided over the daily operation of the paper from 1972 to 1976, wrote critically of some city projects. Specific stories appeared doubting the efficacy of bringing a major league baseball team to Arlington and a project named Seven Seas.[2]

The *Arlington Daily News* repeatedly quoted partisans on both sides of these two issues. Blaser said, "Arlington was not used to controversy. It was a very homogeneous town at the time. My columns, occasionally doubting the wisdom of some projects, were met with strong reaction from many townspeople."[3]

The Atmosphere 17

Mayor B.C. Barnes (8 December 1949).
—*Fort Worth Star-Telegram* Photograph Collection, Special Collections Division
The University of Texas at Arlington Libraries

He remembered that some city council members were furious when he questioned projected attendance figures for the Seven Seas project. He related that the current Mayor Tom Vandergriff wrote letters to the editor about the project and they were published. "Mayor Vandergriff, though differing with me, was always very polite and courteous. Others, however, were less than cordial." [4]

Les Blaser argued in his newspaper column that Seven Seas would drag down other city projects. "Sea-themed sea parks would always have a difficult time in the middle of the state of Texas. Even the *Dallas Morning News* wrote a series of very long articles examining very closely the wisdom and operation of the Seven Seas Park." [5]

Additionally, Blaser argued that the city's bond rating would be adversely affected if the Seven Seas Park failed. The park did eventually falter and close in 1976. Despite having brought in a whale attraction, Newtka the Whale, to spark interest. Even Newtka could not bring life to the theme park.

The *Arlington Daily News* staffers wrote critically long articles on a variety of city projects. The paper also gave prominent coverage to candidates seeking council offices in opposition to incumbents. And its editorials reflected a more independent perspective from that of the dominant establishment.

Eventually, Blaser says, he was eased out of the editor job at the *Arlington Daily News*. "A new publisher came in and wanted the paper to take a more civic-minded booster attitude. I was trained that the practice of journalism was to be highly professional and not be a mouthpiece for the city's leaders. I understood how a growing city like Arlington was still very much a small town politically."[6] Blaser said that he learned much about city politics from the Texas Rangers and Seven Seas projects.

The *Citizen-Journal* also came in for a small amount of criticism from city elites during the debates over city ventures. In 1973 Mayor Vandergriff called upon the publisher of the *Citizen-Journal*, George Hawkes, to convene a meeting of news staffers. The mayor told the assembled staffers of the newsroom to be more "civic minded" and not quote too many citizens opposed to city projects. After the assemblage, the newsroom still went on its own way. "Neither the publisher, George Hawkes, nor his brother Charles Hawkes (a top executive of the paper) put any pressure on the newsroom."[7]

The *Fort Worth Star-Telegram* also covered Arlington events and eventually moved to invest heavily in the *Citizen-Journal*. In 1970 the *Star-Telegram* was having labor problems. The *Citizen-Journal* had a large and sophisticated printing plant on its site on Abrams Street in Arlington. The *Star-Telegram* viewed this investment as a possible back-up in case labor problems interfered at any time with its printing.[8]

The *Star-Telegram* also viewed the *Arlington Daily News* and Belo Corporation as making inroads into Arlington. This also was a factor in their *Citizen-Journal* investment.[9]

In the late 1990s, Belo Corporation would again establish a newspaper here. This time it would have a name close to that of its *Dallas Morning News*. It would be the *Arlington Morning News*. It was to be sold separately, but also be included as a part of the *Dallas Morning News* to its subscribers.

The Atmosphere

The social make-up of the community in the immediate post-World War II years was very homogeneous. It was mostly white and Protestant. There was a small Catholic community, and a very tiny number of Jewish households. A very small African American community was located in a separate geographical area immediately north of the defined downtown area, and referred to as "The Hill."

There were two banks in the community. One was the First National Bank and the other was the Arlington State Bank. They too would be important parts of the economic, political, and social pattern of Arlington, Texas.

The two banks would be competitive on economic matters, but very supportive of the same civic projects and political agenda. The controlling interests in these two banks were longstanding Arlington families, the Cravenses (First National) and the Wilemons (Arlington State).

The patriarch of the Cravens family, Carlisle Cravens, lived next door to the patriarch of the Vandergriff family, Mr. W.T. "Hooker" Vandergriff. This geographic closeness was a representation of the political and social consensus between establishment figures early on.

Howard Wilemon, prominent Arlington banker (21 March 1979).
—Fort Worth Star-Telegram Photograph Collection
Special Collections Division
The University of Texas at Arlington Libraries

Chapter Three

The Vandergriff Years

From the early years of the twentieth century, many towns in Texas had a paternalistic form of governing. One generation of leaders had passed power from one set of leaders to another. At the end of World War II there was no paternalistic pattern in Arlington, Texas.[1] No generation of leaders had emerged to pass power from one generation to the next. But all this would change when Tom J. Vandergriff emerged to become its first real patriarch of political power.

The year 1951 in this study has been designated as a very important year for one major reason. This was when Tom J. Vandergriff, known by his friends as Tommy, became mayor. His tenure in office was to last until 1977.

Early in that year, January 11, 1977, he voluntarily relinquished the office, having served the longest mayoral term in the city's history and one of the longest tenures in the country.

His importance to the development and course of the city cannot be overestimated. In 1986 private citizens organized a fund drive to honor him. A life-size bronze statue was commissioned and dedicated in 1987. The city council authorized the placing of the statue in the lobby of the Arlington City Hall.

Tom Vandergriff (15 November 1960).
—*Fort Worth Star-Telegram* Photograph Collection
Special Collections Division
The University of Texas at Arlington Libraries

Additionally, a large park in south central Arlington is named Vandergriff Park. And the Arlington Memorial Hospital, for which his family donated land, has a large structure with the Vandergriff name as well.

The new Ballpark in Arlington, which houses the Texas Rangers baseball team, has a Vandergriff Pavilion. The ball club announced in 1996 that a sculpture of Tom Vandergriff would be placed in a prominent place within the Ballpark, and it was completed a few years later. Seldom has a community paid such homage to a political figure.

The Ballpark honor is to commemorate the influence and tenacity with which Tom Vandergriff and his father, W.T.

"Hooker" Vandergriff, brought the Washington Senators to Arlington. Later the team was renamed the Texas Rangers.

The Washington Senators' principal owner, Bob Short, was in financial difficulty. Mayor Vandergriff in a bold move made overtures to locate the Senators to Arlington. At the time, major league baseball teams made their homes in the principal cities of the nation. Arlington in 1970, when the baseball negotiations were underway, had a population of 90,392—far smaller than New York, Chicago, and Washington D.C. of the day.

The financial arrangement to bring the Senators to Arlington was guaranteed by "Hooker" Vandergriff, the mayor's father. Hooker Vandergriff had always been a fan of baseball and this was his chance to bring his "field of dreams" to fruition.

The city would purchase the radio and television rights of the baseball team for ten years. Bob Short was being loaned money by banks to alleviate his financial problems, and Hooker Vandergriff guaranteed the bank loans. Bob Short eventually paid back the loans, which had been guaranteed; however, it was indeed a large financial risk undertaken by the Vandergriff patriarch. Bob Short benefited by getting out of debt. Arlington benefited by bringing a major league ball team to town.

It would be the last time a baseball franchise would be transferred to another city. There would be expansion teams, but no transfers from this time on.[2] The Washington Senators officially came to Arlington in 1971 and played their first game as the Texas Rangers in April 1972.

W.T. Vandergriff, nicknamed "Hooker" after a Civil War general, had been a longtime General Motors automobile dealer. He had maintained dealerships in Carrollton, Texas, and Irving, Texas. In 1937 he opened a dealership in Arlington and relocated his home residence and principal business interests to the Arlington community.

In addition to "Hooker" Vandergriff's General Motors automobile dealership in Arlington, he also operated an appliance and a furniture business at times.

Tom Vandergriff, like many political leaders, possessed

oratorical skills. His speechmaking ability became legendary in the community. At an early age these skills would command the attention of the then small Arlington business and professional community.

After graduating from high school, Tom was enrolled at Northwestern University, a university known for its excellent forensics program. A very young Tom Vandergriff early on wanted a career as a radio or sports announcer.

Later he transferred to the University of Southern California. His goal still was to be a news broadcaster to utilize his skills. As a student he auditioned with a national broadcast network for an announcer job. The management was impressed with his voice and skills, but gave the job to another young man, Chet Huntley. Mr. Huntley went on to national television newscaster fame as part of the "Huntley and Brinkley" duo on NBC.

While attending the University of Southern California, Vandergriff was able to travel and analyze the newly emerging California lifestyle of suburban living. The emerging entertainment culture and expanding population of California in the post-World War II years influenced him greatly.

He would bring back those impressions of California to Arlington. In later years, as Arlington grew and the entertainment theme of the city was imprinted, Arlington would be compared to Anaheim, California.

Arlington's demographic future would not be tied to its small downtown area. Political leaders under the guidance of Tom Vandergriff would work to expand the city in many directions. It would aggressively annex available land.

The city's original master plan called for commercial districts in various parts of the municipality. This tended toward regional centers, which would become part of Arlington's identity.[3] This planned strategy would make it difficult to sustain a downtown area as the city developed and expanded in coming years.

In 1949 Tom Vandergriff, then twenty-three years old, became the head of the very tiny Arlington Chamber of Commerce. He held this position from 1949 to 1951. This would help him make the acquaintances and gain the confidence of business leaders.

Early on, the Arlington Chamber of Commerce would serve as an important rallying point for the city's economic development. From the late 1940s until the end of the century, chamber officers and members would play an active role in city politics.[4]

In 1951, at the age of twenty-five, Tom Vandergriff would run for mayor against the incumbent mayor, B.C. Barnes.

There was no animosity between the two candidates. But there was a larger reason for Vandergriff's decision to challenge the incumbent mayor.

A bit earlier it became known that General Motors Corporation was searching for a place to establish an automobile assembly plant. If General Motors would establish an assembly plant in Arlington, it would be a major step in the growth that some Arlington decision-makers had hoped for.

Grand Prairie, close neighbor to the east and with whom Arlington had always been compared, had a naval air station since 1942. After Arlington Downs racetrack closed in 1936, many Arlington leaders were looking to attract a large corporation or defense plant to the city.[5] Bringing General Motors to Arlington would be a major step in this direction.

Attracting large enterprises to an area was much different in the early 1950s than forty years later. Today corporations or government enterprises conduct extensive and very professional studies in addition to the more informal and political ties that may pertain.

In earlier years, attracting such institutions was almost entirely a matter of personal acquaintance, word-of-mouth, or political ties. The Vandergriff family ties to General Motors as a longtime automobile franchise holder would now prove useful both for the city and for Tom Vandergriff.

It was felt that if Tom Vandergriff could become mayor it would instill a certain degree of confidence in General Motors establishing an assembly plant. General Motors executives knew the Vandergriff family and of their longtime association with the corporation. Attracting General Motors to Arlington would be the primary motive in a very young Tom Vandergriff's decision as a mayoral candidate.

There is anecdotal information that Tom Vandergriff was

encouraged to run by a group of influential Arlington citizens. They recognized the energy and potential he had plus the advantage of his father's considerable political and economic strength.[6]

Tom Vandergriff has denied that he was ever approached by a group of influential Arlington citizens at the time.[7] Regardless, Arlington's early decision-makers were anxious to support the young mayoral candidate after his decision to run.

Tom Vandergriff at the age of twenty-five defeated B.C. Barnes and became the new mayor on April 3, 1951. It was not an especially hard-fought contest. There were no campaign expense-reporting requirements, but best estimates put most contributions between five and ten dollars. Each candidate spent about one hundred dollars total during the political campaign.

There were no hard feelings between the two contenders after the election. Later a city park was dedicated in the name of former Mayor Barnes.

And in the summer of 1951, General Motors made a decision to establish a plant in Arlington, Texas! Mayor Vandergriff and his father, "Hooker" Vandergriff, then went about personally purchasing parcels of land at market value to pave the way for the General Motors location.[8] In 1953 the plant opened and has been a pivotal feature in Arlington's economic and political life ever since.

Tom Vandergriff became known as the "Boy" mayor and would share that title with another young man who was elected about the same time as mayor of Weatherford, Texas. His name was Jim Wright, later to become a United States Congressman and Speaker of the United States House of Representatives.

Now Tom Vandergriff, the "Boy" mayor, was to assemble an informal group of leaders who would chart the course of the community for many years.

Arlington Leaders Forge Elite Governance

Arlington, Texas, during the era examined was dominated politically by a small group of individuals. In what is defined as the elitist theory of government, this group came to governing positions, elected or non-elected, by their wealth, reputation, personality, or business prominence.

This study will attempt to place the Arlington political arena into an elitist conceptual framework. Though most political leaders in Arlington, Texas, as in other places, repeatedly talked about participatory democracy, it was in fact governed by a few.

Perhaps Harold Lasswell, one of the early greats of American political science, said it best. "Government is always government by the few, whether in the name of the few, the one, or the many."[9]

The elitist theory of government goes against what many people believe about government. Many believe that all governmental units are run, to paraphrase Abraham Lincoln, "of the people, by the people, and for the people." Many civics lessons and speeches extol how the average citizen can affect change, how everybody can reach and attain any high public office. Further, the importance of voting, the importance of political participation in the community, is always stressed by politicians and the media.

Even though elite theory holds that governments are run by a few, democratic principles and practices can still be employed and practiced. There need be no conspiratorial aspect to this theory. No secret cabal.

Ironically, many elites hold democratic principles and practices more strongly than do the masses. The theory holds that the very apathy of the masses allows for democratic principles to flourish.

Democratic principles involve much more than participatory acts like voting. They entail an attachment to principles like tolerance and adherence to individual rights. Studies reveal that it is the elites, rather than the masses, which hold these tenets most strongly.[10]

Elite rule is common in state and local politics. It is perhaps more pronounced at this level than any other. Arlington was not unique in this respect.

Thomas Dye and Harmon Zeigler agree, "The masses play an even smaller role in state and local politics than they do in national politics. The news media emphasize national politics rather than state or community politics. Very few citizens know who their state senator or state representative is or who their city council members or county commissioners are. We can expect 50 percent of the nation's eligible voters to cast ballots in presidential elections, but turnout in state gubernatorial elections in nonpresidential years is generally less than 50 percent. Municipal elections often attract fewer than 20 to 30 percent of the eligible voters."[11] Arlington voters through the period of this study fit largely into this framework.

In the larger Texas cities, elite rule often has been in the form of organizations specifically constituted to influence and direct. For many years Dallas has had a group of influential citizens in an organization called the Dallas Citizens Council.

The Dallas Citizens Council was organized in 1937. Its power and influence became legendary. Studied extensively by Carol Estes Thometz in 1963, this work was one of the first to examine how a powerful, small group directed Dallas' civic and political life.[12]

Likewise, Houston, San Antonio, and Fort Worth all have had similar organizations although some were more loosely structured than that of Dallas. San Antonio had an organization called the Good Government League. Its composition was the leading business executives of the city.

The title "Good Government League" must have had a good ring to it, for El Paso also had a Good Government League, which helped to cement its elite structure. Fort Worth's elite group was more informal—but still very effective—through what was popularly called "The Seventh Street Gang." The title was given to them because many of the executive offices along and near Seventh Street in downtown Fort Worth housed Fort Worth's leadership.

These elite structures and organizations, effective for a half-century or more, have changed their roles. They are more open and diversified. There still may be a form of elite rule, but their authority and dominance is not as pronounced.

The city of Arlington had no formal organization to rival that of the larger Texas cities. But there were elites in Arlington, however loosely organized, who directed the city's future. And they came together under the benevolent but strong leadership of Tom Vandergriff. This leadership cadre was put in place with his election in 1951 and endured for at least two decades, even after his departure from the mayor's office in 1977.

The Emergence of Mayoral Authority

The political importance of Tom Vandergriff cannot be overestimated throughout his mayoral tenure. After Tom Vandergriff's departure as mayor there was some informal discussion among a few Arlington decision-makers about the formation of a more formal and structured organization to fill the political vacuum—modeled on that of Dallas and other Texas cities.

Without Tom Vandergriff at the helm some believed the city might lose its powerful driving force and the consensus he helped to build might erode.[13]

The early 1950s were important to the political career of the young mayor. He was able to prove that even at a young age his political strength was considerable. His early successes established a reputation for political results that would be lasting.

In the 1950s, Arlington began to exhibit some of the growth and expansion that would be its political hallmark for several generations to come. In 1953 it added another major park and named it Randol Mill Park. It was only the second major park in the city after Meadowbrook Park, which had been constructed with a swimming pool years earlier.

Also in 1953, a new police station was built, and a year later a new central fire station was added. But the most important addition was the choice by General Motors to establish a new assembly plant in the city. With this addition to the city, bringing with it thousands of new workers and residents over the years, the city's growth was assured and Tom Vandergriff's political stature enhanced.

Prior to Tom Vandergriff's role as mayor, refunding contracts were used to augment the city's growth pattern and attract developers to build homes for new workers, thus a unique funding mechanism was put in place. "Refunding contracts were agreements between the city and the developer for the city to reimburse the contractor the cost of the infrastructure."[14] Refunding contracts were established in the late 1940s, used extensively in the 1950s, and phased out entirely in the 1960s.

The policy of refunding was a direct predecessor to the often-controversial policies of tax rebates and public-private ventures of later years. Revenue from water bills was the principal source of refunding. Lynda Gayda Miller in her research at the University of Texas at Arlington concluded in a study that "Clearly, two arguments can be made about refunding contracts: the largest population percentage increase in Arlington's history occurred during the time they were being used, and although a higher number of people moved to Arlington in other decades, the 1950s growth started the momentum of the phenomenal growth experience."[15]

At a conference of city managers from the state of Texas held in Dallas in 1953, it was recognized that Arlington was the only city in the state to be using refunding contracts. It stimulated a broad-based discussion of the mechanism, with Arlington defending its use.[16]

The political strength and powerful legend of Tom Vandergriff was knit together with his mayoral role. Those who grew up with him, attended high school with him, or became close political allies would refer to him always and affectionately as "Tommy." To others, he was "The Mayor."

Of medium build and about five feet eight inches in height, he was always impeccably and conservatively dressed. Rarely would he appear even at informal occasions without wearing a suit and tie.

These two parts, his extraordinary political and social skills coupled with the mayor's office, gave him relatively the political strength of the big city mayors of New York City, Chicago, Boston, and Philadelphia. His reputation as mayor of Arlington became known far outside the confines of the city.[17]

Arlington had had a city manager since 1949 even though it maintained the title "commissioner" for its elected municipal officeholders for another decade. Even under the city manager form of government, which designates day-to-day municipal governance to the professional managers, Mayor Vandergriff early on played a daily governing role. This role would be continued throughout his entire tenure in office.[18]

Mayor Vandergriff practiced personal acts of kindness, which endeared him to citizens for a lifetime. He would write personal notes to citizens thanking them for their interest in various civic and city matters.

As an unintended consequence, these notes and other beneficent acts on his part would knit together a loyal cadre of supporters. Mayor Vandergriff to many was not just an ordinary elected official. He knew many people's history, when they came to town, their occupations, births, and deaths.

The author remembers, in the early 1970s, seeing him at the small graveside funeral of the wife of a beloved Arlington State College faculty member. This was not a political act. It was an act of loyalty, of remembrance, as a close friend or family member would do. As mayor, as the leader of the Arlington community, he had also become a part of their families and they of his.

Mayor Vandergriff exhibited civic pride and welcome at realtor open house sales. In the 1950s, as the population grew, the mayor would help to greet prospective homebuyers. This was a great help to realtors, a welcome to new arrivals, and an example of his mastery of politics at a personal level.

When he became a mayor, Arlington was a very small place. But his attention to detail and fondness for people would prove beneficial as Arlington grew into a much larger and more complex society. His early base of support and loyalty would stay with him and grow.

And like a beloved family member, any perceived criticism of him would evoke scorn from his many allies. One city council contender remembers visiting an important Arlington realtor in the late 1970s to gain support. Before he could even begin his presentation, the realtor remarked that no criticism of the mayor would be heard. Ironically, the would-be council member had no intention of criticizing the mayor.[19]

The Vandergriff family would make both large and small

donations of money, property, and goods to charitable groups and to schools. As a political leader he would address and mediate citizen complaints ranging from the simple to the extraordinary, which under a strict city manager system would be taken care of by the manager and staff.

Real or imagined, many longtime citizens would relate stories of how Mayor Vandergriff personally presented a solution to a problem. The reminiscences ranged from obtaining a much needed neighborhood street light to re-scheduling for a missed trash pickup. He has been given credit through numerous tales for his kindnesses, from rescuing stranded cats in trees to making sure street potholes were filled.

For many citizens Mayor Vandergriff became the center of their civic lives. Whether or not some of the tales about his personal diligence were mythical or not, he was called on directly by citizens for a myriad of problems and projects. Over the years this would establish a powerful political constituency.

Early on, he began to utilize his unique and resonating voice, not just at political and civic events, but also as a sports announcer at sporting events. For many years he announced the Arlington High School home football games. Later he would announce the football games of Arlington State College and the University of Texas at Arlington. Fans were always delighted to hear his booming voice reverberate with expressions like: "He was tackled just short of the goal line but there is a question on the play." He too delighted in this voluntary, non-compensatory, sports announcing position. Home football fans became accustomed to and delighted in this unique informal mayoral role.

It is difficult to separate the many informal beneficent acts of Mayor Vandergriff from his more official duties as they overlapped considerably. And these beneficial acts endured long after he had vacated the mayor's office.

In the early 1980s, while serving in the United States Congress, he visited a very elderly woman named Louise Leatherman on a fact-finding mission. In Congress he had become interested in the problems of aging.

While visiting the elderly Arlington resident, they began

to discuss baseball. Baseball was always of particular interest to the Vandergriff family. The woman's brother, nicknamed "Roasty" Appleton, had been a pitcher for the former Brooklyn Dodgers and was the "toast" of Arlington when the Vandergriff family first arrived in the community.

The woman remarked that she remembered an old photo of her major league baseball brother with other players, but did not know of its whereabouts. Several weeks later, Tom Vandergriff presented her with the newly framed photo he had located.

Louise "Susie" Leatherman was 105 years of age at the time of the Vandergriff visit. She had lived in the community longer than any other person at that point and was a great source of stories for this study. Her husband was the town's first postal deliveryman. The Appleton family has a small street named for them in the central part of the city.

Mayor Vandergriff never forgot those who helped him realize city goals. A private citizen early in the 1950s voluntarily helped in the General Motors plant location. It involved a land transaction crucial to the plant's water needs.

While mayor and even after leaving office, he would routinely remember citizens with personal acts of kindness long into that person's old age.

Throughout the 1950s, Tom Vandergriff's popularity and political support solidified. The city council (still referred to as commissioners until July 1960) was very stable. Some commissioners would be elected and re-elected for a decade or more.

A consensus pivoting upon growth and stability was being established. A unity among the political elite was being forged. Real estate, business, and professional interests were generally of one political voice. They may have differed on the details, but the basic movement was agreed upon. Arlington would pursue a path of growth to be recognized as something other than a small suburban "bedroom" community. This elite consensus would form the bedrock upon which most future political decisions would be formed.

In some communities where a large college or university might be located, a chasm could develop. University professors and students would form one political block and those in the broader community another. This became generally known as the "town versus gown" controversy.

In Arlington, Texas, this "town versus gown" controversy would not develop. Only in the 1970s would there be any hint of such a split. Even then the political differences were more of perception than reality.

The presidents of Arlington State College and later of the University of Texas at Arlington never voiced any disapproval of city leaders' goals. Both the city and university leadership would serve each other's agendas well.

Especially in the 1950s and 1960s, university personnel were members of civic groups like the Optimist, Kiwanis, and Rotary. Many university personnel were members of the city's largest churches, which had city leaders as its members as well. They banked at the city's two largest financial institutions, and a few were involved with various business interests in the city.

In the 1950s and 1960s some university professors were very active in university policy-making and were known as activists in the broader community's life as well. One professor and administrator, E.C. Barksdale, and his wife, Marge, were influential in county and state politics as well as having an interest in city politics.

Continually during the 1950s and 1960s, E.C. Barksdale held a weekly Friday afternoon get-together at his home. Invitees included both city and university people. They would exchange ideas in a relaxed atmosphere away from university or city offices.

City leaders often assisted the university in its many changes from a two-year to a four-year college. As well, they helped in the transition to a senior university and finally into the University of Texas System. The assistance to the university in its early struggles to become a major university was considerable.[20]

The governor of Texas at the time, John Connally, helped the university move from the Texas A&M System into the University of Texas System. Earlier, there was some consideration whether the university should stand alone with its own regents and governance or become a part of the University of Texas System, which it eventually did.

The Arlington Chamber of Commerce would occasionally hold receptions honoring high administrative officials at the university. University administrators came to realize early on that the growth of Arlington as a city would help them attain their goals as a major state university.

And for most of the 1950s and into the early 1960s a professor, H.A.D. Dunsworth, served on the city council. He was both a respected university professor and an influential Arlington citizen.

In 1977 Samuel Hamlett, the chairman of the political science department at the University of Texas at Arlington, was elected to the council. In 1987 Larry Walther, a faculty member in the College of Business, was elected.

Samuel Hamlett served one term before being defeated by Leo Berman in a run-off election. Larry Walther served two terms and then chose not to run again.

There was usually smooth sailing between the university and community leaders; however, there were a few tense periods. Those developed primarily when the city was embroiled in controversies surrounding the proposed implementation of single-member districts and city support of a major league ballpark.

In the late 1970s a group of city leaders visited university officials and asked that Del Taebel, a professor of the School of Urban Affairs, be fired. The allegation was that Professor Taebel had utilized university facilities to expound his views on single-member districts. The allegations were denied.

The university refused to fire the professor on the grounds that academic freedom protected his right to speak and write on any subject.[21]

There were other instances where university personnel drew criticism from city leaders. Another professor in the School of Urban Affairs, Marc Rosentraub, had written extensively on sports venues and their economic impact on communities. His analysis of the economic issues of ballparks did not equate with that of city leaders.

There was never any demand that Professor Rosentraub be removed from his university position, but his studies did cause concern and criticism from some city leaders.

Still another instance in the same time period involved the author of this study. A University of Texas at Arlington athletic booster who had supported the athletic program monetarily in the past threatened to discontinue his support unless the author stopped writing in favor of single-member districts in a local newspaper.

The author was told of the donor's threats to discontinue funding by information relayed from top athletic department personnel. The name of the irate athletic donor was never given even though requested.

Regardless of conflicts, the consensus among the elites prepared the city for future growth. This is not to say that there was no opposition to growth projects. There were those, in a political minority, who wished to retain the status quo or proceed more slowly. But their arguments did not fully become part of the elite conversation.

The lack of a formal organization of community leaders like that which existed in Dallas and a few other Texas cities did nothing to hinder Arlington's political visionaries. Mayor Tom Vandergriff provided ideas for projects, which other community leaders supported and joined. In a more diverse environment a structured political organization may have been necessary. But at the time there was a strong consensus on what needed to be done. No structural entity was needed.[22]

The city's major banks, Arlington State and First National were never hostile toward one another. Arlington State Bank was formed in 1937, while First National opened in 1952. From their early founding, they competed with one another but never broke ranks over larger city goals as they arose.

This cooperative political atmosphere between the two banks contributed to city growth, according to George Hawkes.[23] In Arlington's neighboring city, Grand Prairie, the major banks, Grand Prairie State and First National Bank of Grand Prairie, were often split over major political topics and the city's direction for at least the decades from the 1940s to the 1960s.[24]

Land in the early days of the community was a primary source of wealth. How the land was to be utilized, zoned, and made attractive to investors was paramount. Banking loans to developers was central to this process.

Arlington's influential banking community would be at the center of elite interaction. They were in general support of the city's direction and growth. Banking executives would naturally be interested in who was appointed to boards dealing with zoning and development and who was elected to city council and mayoral posts.

Arlington's two major banks were directed for the most part by two of the city's oldest and most prominent families: the Wilemon family with Arlington State and the Cravens family with First National.[25] Both the Wilemon family and the Cravens family were closely allied from the start with the Vandergriff family.

As previously referenced, the Cravens family residence was next door to that of W.T. "Hooker" Vandergriff's family. Carlisle Cravens, the patriarch of the Cravens family, was a close friend of the Vandergriffs as were Claude Wilemon, patriarch of the Wilemon family, and his son, Howard Wilemon, who eventually became chairman of the board of First National Bank.

The closest mechanism to a formal political alliance was one loosely formed by the Arlington Chamber of Commerce, Arlington Board of Realtors, First National Bank, Arlington State Bank, Arlington State College, Arlington *Citizen-Journal* newspaper, and several civic groups—the most prominent being the downtown Arlington Rotary Club.

Most of Arlington's civic club charters prohibited active political endorsements or support of candidates. Yet there was an informal kind of endorsement that prevailed, especially with the Downtown Rotary Club, which met at the First United Methodist Church.

This group was one of the oldest civic clubs in the city, dating back to 1923. The membership included representatives from every major city profession and business. At various times several city council members would be active Rotarians as well.[26] This club provided an intersecting point for community leaders.

Legends grew up about the political strength of the

Downtown Rotary. Perhaps some of the perceived strength was imagined, but nevertheless political aspirants sought out Downtown Rotary members for individual support.

Only once did the major civic groups formally endorse a candidate for city council. That was in 1975, when at least ten civic clubs endorsed Carolyn Snider with a political endorsement in the Arlington *Citizen-Journal*.

Depending on the politics of the day, the loose coalition of interest groups would organize their membership to support proposals such as bond issues. Some organizations would hold forums to introduce their members to city council candidates. Later, a favored technique of some groups would be telephone phone banks to rally citizens to vote.

As political campaigns became more organized, troops of supporters would campaign outside of the two major banks. Handing out campaign cards or brochures to passers-by became a tradition. Political advertisements in the Arlington *Citizen-Journal* backing a particular candidate became commonplace. Readers would search for the important names for clues as to which way the political establishment was inclined.

City politics would later become more sophisticated in electioneering. At times paid public relations companies would run political campaigns and bond issue proposals. Various brochures would be designed and mailed to constituents, and endorsement cards became common.

Another legacy grew up from the early days of Arlington city politics. Aspiring political candidates and their friends routinely would consult with Mayor Tom Vandergriff for his support.

This practice did not originate with the mayor, but as his perceived and actual political prowess increased, informal consultation with him became common. He would always remain noncommittal with newcomers, listening politely, but refusing to endorse anyone outside of the council incumbents up for re-election.

Mayor Vandergriff was always consistent in supporting council incumbents. If an incumbent council member was opposed for re-election, the telephone banks and informal coalition of establishment interests would go into gear.

Maxine Roane, a longtime friend and political ally of Mayor Vandergriff, remembers organizing numerous political telephone banks. These telephone banks, staffed by volunteers, were primarily drawn from real estate firms. No one was paid, although a few real estate employees may have felt a bit of coercion to participate. Mostly the telephone banks were located in local real estate offices.[27] The many real estate offices at the time of expansive growth, both commercial and residential, were firmly aligned with the growth policies of the city.

The traditional opening sentence for phone callers would be "I am calling for Tom Vandergriff and would appreciate your support for council member..." The intended effect of course was to convey to the person called that Mayor Vandergriff was supporting the incumbent. Nearly all of the time this support would go a long way to a successful outcome.[28]

Mayor Vandergriff's office at the family Chevrolet dealership, at the intersection of two heavily traveled streets, was marked by a huge letter "V" in front of the building. It became the commonly accepted place for him to meet with political aspirants. The large "V" sign was later moved to Vandergriff

Maxine Roane and Victor Vandergriff (15 September 1995).
—Photo courtesy of Maxine Roane

The Vandergriff Years

Park after the sale of the dealership. Mayor Vandergriff's business office at the dealership became associated as much with Arlington politics as did city hall. In addition to the political aspirants, citizens with all sorts of complaints, requests, and pleadings would wait to meet with the mayor personally.

Interestingly, ten years after Tom Vandergriff had left office, Richard Greene, who became mayor in 1987, occupied the same office at the Chevrolet dealership for a short time.[29] However, there was seldom the number of people waiting to plead their political cause outside his office. Nevertheless, this is a striking reminder of the continuity that permeated Arlington city politics at the time.

During the mid to late 1950s, Arlington politics, under the leadership of Tom Vandergriff, set the stage for subsequent Arlington growth and development. In 1956 a development in the eastern sector of the city named Great Southwest Development was begun. Angus Wynne, who has been credited with forming the Six Flags Amusement Park, also was instrumental in developing Great Southwest.

This area became a grouping of regional and national warehouses and distribution centers, which extended the name recognition, economic vitality, and tax base of the city. James Knapp, a longtime Arlington businessman, attorney, and entrepreneur, believed that this development was the catalyst and perhaps one of the most important signposts in the city's history.[30]

Along with Angus Wynne, Bill Zeckendorf, a prominent New York investor, was instrumental in the early development of the Great Southwest Industrial Park. James Knapp credits this investor as an important figure in Arlington's development through his interest in this enterprise.[31]

In early 1957, the Dallas-Fort Worth Turnpike was opened. This turnpike, later to be renamed Interstate 30 after the turnpike bonds were retired, was critical to bringing other businesses to Arlington.

Arlington's support of the Dallas-Fort Worth Turnpike idea when first proposed was very important. Again, under the leadership of Tom Vandergriff and his political supporters, groundwork was laid for future expansion of the city.

James "Big Daddy" Knapp—Political observer, activist, and prominent landowner (21 March 1979).

—Fort Worth Star-Telegram
Photograph Collection
Special Collections Division
The University of
Texas at Arlington Libraries

To gain Arlington's unqualified support of the new turnpike, the necessary political backing was garnered to construct an East-West roadway connection to Grand Prairie. This would eventually become Highway 303, known in Arlington as Pioneer Parkway.

For backing of the turnpike between Dallas and Fort Worth, support in the 1950s was obtained for the newly proposed Interstate 20 to include much of then rural south Arlington in its route. Conceptualized during the infancy of the interstate highway system, Interstate 20 was completed several decades later. It has been a major traffic artery for the entire region and has brought economic benefits to Arlington.

As Arlington's growth proceeded, a reliable and continual source of water became important. The city was especially mindful of the concerns of larger businesses like General Motors for water.

When a proposal to construct a reservoir was made, small controversies ensued. A few residents questioned the money to be spent, while others recognized that this reservoir would likely spur more growth.

The Vandergriff Years

The question of how and whether the new reservoir would obtain and hold water was of concern to some. In 1957, during an extremely heavy and continual rainfall, the new reservoir opened. It was filled in twenty-seven days, and Lake Arlington became another of the legendary tales in the political portfolio of Tom Vandergriff.

In 1958, beginning with a Vandergriff family donation of land, Arlington Memorial Hospital opened. The donated land originally was to be a home place for the family. But its location, then at the periphery of town, was perfect for a new community hospital and so the donation was made.

After the land donation, the entire community, small as it was then, began a drive for money to construct the hospital. Tom Vandergriff's sister, Ginger Vandergriff Deering, helped to lead the hospital fund drive in the community.[32]

Again it was another in the many donations and activities binding the Vandergriff family to the community. This continued the overlapping of the political life of Mayor Tom Vandergriff and the public and charitable works of his family.

In 1960 Six Flags Over Texas was opened. The fledgling tourism industry, which would become part of Arlington's identity, was launched. The business of entertainment would bring tax dollars to Arlington as well as a ripple effect in the local economy with spending by tourists on food, clothing, and shelter.

Angus Wynne, a prominent Dallas developer, was instrumental in this project. In late 1999, Highway 360, on the east side of the city, was renamed the "Angus Wynne Freeway" in his honor. This name designation was done at the urging of Tom Vandergriff, who at this time was a county judge presiding over the Tarrant County Commissioners' Court.

In the late 1950s, the opening of the Dallas-Fort Worth Turnpike made Six Flags Over Texas a perfect fit between Dallas and Fort Worth. Now, with the Great Southwest Industrial District and Six Flags, Arlington's political leaders could not only boast of its location midway between the two cities, but could cite evidence that its location could attract national businesses.

Not surprisingly, the city council from the mid-1950s and for the next several decades would be mostly business and developer oriented. Representatives of some of the city's largest businesses were represented.

Automobile dealerships, banking, commercial and residential development were always heavily represented on the council and on the city's premier citizen board, the Planning and Zoning Commission. With only a few exceptions there was a general consensus on city goals.

Many of the council members would serve multiple consecutive terms, usually three. Rarely would an incumbent council member be defeated in a general election. Most incumbents vacated their council positions voluntarily after serving these multiple consecutive terms. Those taking their place on the council would continue in the same political direction as their predecessors.

H.A.D. Dunsworth served consecutive terms on the council from 1953 to 1963. He was a professor at Arlington State College, but also was on the board of a local bank. Dixon Purvis, a businessman, served consecutive terms on the council from 1955 to 1963. Charles E.C. Brown, who was in the lumber business, served consecutively from 1965 to 1971.

Willard Sutton served from 1966 to 1972. Doland Maner, an executive with Southern Industrial Steel Company in Arlington, served from 1967 to 1975. John Ball, an attorney, was elected to consecutive terms from 1964 to 1970. Dr. R.G. "Wick" Alexander, a local orthodontist, served from 1971 to 1977.

Perhaps best illustrative of the stability and continuity of city politics would be four names: Tom Vandergriff, S.J. Stovall, Harold Patterson, and Richard Greene. Tom Vandergriff retained the mayor's office from 1951 to 1977. S.J. Stovall, an employee of the Corps of Engineers, was a council member from 1963 to 1977 when he assumed the office of mayor after the voluntary resignation of Tom Vandergriff. S.J. Stovall remained mayor until 1983 and then chose not to run again for re-election. Harold Patterson, a local banker, was a member of the council consecutively from 1966 to 1983. In 1983 he was elected as mayor and remained in the office until

1987. Richard Greene, a local savings and loan executive and later part owner of an automobile business, was elected to consecutive terms on the council from 1984 to 1987 when he was elected mayor. He served as mayor until 1997. Altogether these four men served a total of eighty years in one capacity or another on the council.

Chapter Four

Post Vandergriff: Continuity and Growth with Three Mayors

On January 11, 1977, without any advance warning or even political rumor circulating, Tom Vandergriff voluntarily relinquished the mayor's chair. He had been mayor for twenty-six years. Most people in the community had never known another mayor.

There were very few people in the council chambers the evening of the resignation. Mayor Vandergriff had talked to S.J. Stovall, who was mayor pro tempore, earlier on the telephone, but said nothing about resignation. "He (Vandergriff) was almost nostalgic, but gave no hint of resignation."[1]

The evening of the resignation, S.J. Stovall was out of town in San Francisco on a business trip for the Corps of Engineers. In the hotel room where they were staying Mrs. Stovall answered the telephone and was informed that her husband was now the acting mayor of Arlington.

Dr. R.G. "Wick" Alexander, who was on the council at the time, remembers that Mayor Vandergriff would usually make a few remarks at the end of every council meeting. The evening of his resignation he began to make his usual after the

Tom Vandergriff soon after his resignation as mayor (13 January 1977).
—*Fort Worth Star-Telegram* Photograph Collection
Special Collections Division
The University of Texas at Arlington Libraries

meeting comments. Most council members relaxed to hear some remarks on new projects or whatever, but had no indication of what the mayor would begin to say.

The mayor mentioned that he had seen the Broadway play "Chorus Line" and began to recite some of the lines, "What I did, I did for love" (in a reference to his long tenure as mayor).[2]

Then the mayor continued, "I'll miss each of you, and I'll miss this room, it's the most beautiful room in the world to me. But I'm absolutely convinced the heartbreak for me would be a thousand times greater if I finished my term." The council members were stunned by the announcement. The mayor broke a bit of the gloom and emotion of the moment by adding, "Besides, can you really see Tom Vandergriff as a lame-duck mayor?"[3]

Mayor Vandergriff left the meeting. The council adjourned and would not speak to the press immediately. They then traveled a short distance and met informally at the International House of Pancakes to discuss what to do with Mayor Vandergriff no longer serving as mayor.[4]

After the mayor's abrupt resignation there was, among some community leaders, a fear that a political vacuum would result. There was repeated discussion about forming a more structured leadership organization modeled after the Dallas Citizen's Council, but the idea never materialized.

What did occur in the late 1970s was discussion of and eventual creation in 1980 of an organization called Leadership Arlington. It was modeled on a Fort Worth organization, Leadership Fort Worth. It was to educate and acquaint younger promising adults, many already in community leadership roles, with the structure of city government. Participants were recruited from every sector of the community: the university, philanthropy, health, public schools, business, and the professions.

The overall intent was geared to train new community and political leadership. Dr. R.G. "Wick" Alexander, a past council member, Elwood Preiss, a high-ranking University of Texas at Arlington administrator, and Sally Kallam, an Arlington civic leader, were instrumental in creating Leadership Arlington, which remained active two decades later with over 5,000 participants by the end of the 1990s.

Mayor Vandergriff had timed his resignation so that there would be no need to call a special election to fill the office. Mayor pro-tempore Stovall could take over as acting mayor until the regular election schedule came due.

After his abrupt and surprising resignation as mayor, Tom Vandergriff would not make any comments for several days thereafter. Mayor Stovall remembers that he "could not be found."[5] Most likely the outgoing mayor did not wish to detract attention from the new mayor and council and wanted to let them get on with the city's business.

After S.J. Stovall assumed the office of mayor, he commented, "That Tom Vandergriff never initiated any conversations about city business. I would occasionally ask his advice and opinion and received some, but only after I (Stovall) initiated the conversation."[6]

Perhaps the most asked question of the day was "Why?" Why would a man (Vandergriff) who had been mayor for so many years abruptly step down without any warning? Perhaps the best answer is a combination of the personal and political.

Tom Vandergriff had never been immersed in the family business. The majority of his time was spent in city politics and civic endeavors. Perhaps, after twenty-six years as mayor, he felt a need to return to the family business.

A longtime acquaintance of the Vandergriff family, Dan Gould, Jr., remembers visiting with "Hooker" Vandergriff, the family patriarch, shortly after the resignation statement. "I will have my son back in business with me," Dan Gould, Jr. remembers Hooker Vandergriff as saying.[7]

S.J. Stovall had been Mayor Vandergriff's longtime friend and ally. He was always the loyal and trusted companion on the council. By leaving office at this time, Vandergriff would allow S.J. Stovall to assume the office for a while and make it easier for him (Stovall) to be re-elected in a future election.

If Mayor Vandergriff had simply announced his intention of not running for mayor during the next election cycle, the mayoral election may have opened up in a way he did not wish.

By leaving the office abruptly he would not have to endure continuing questioning about his motives. Also, if there is a duty or obligation to perform that is not too pleasant, it may be better to do it quickly and get it out of the way.

Others, however, have cited a variety of reasons for Mayor Vandergriff's hasty political departure after so many years of service. Les Blaser, former editor of the *Arlington Daily News,* has speculated that it had something to do with the failure of the Seven Seas venture. "This was his only real political failure. Its failure may have compromised Arlington's bond rating a bit. Possibly, some financial institutions may have wished the city to cease its speculation in such enterprises."[8]

Seven Seas pivoted upon a sea-life tourism theme. It was launched in 1972 and closed down in 1975. The Arlington Convention Center is now located on some of the land that Seven Seas once occupied.

S.J. Stovall took over as mayor of a town that had only

Mayor Vandergriff with Mike Jenkins and Seven Seas design model (13 January 1977).
—Fort Worth Star-Telegram Photograph Collection
Special Collections Division
The University of Texas at Arlington Libraries

known Tom Vandergriff. It would be a daunting task. But he would continue to provide stable and sound leadership. Mayor Stovall, a very soft-spoken, mild-mannered man, offered a likeness to his predecessor—he was always conservatively attired in a business suit. His friends and acquaintances would usually refer to him by his first initials, "S.J."

He came to Arlington in 1950 and worked for the United States Corps of Engineers. Very quickly he became active in community affairs. He joined the First Baptist Church and became one of its stalwart members.

In 1961 local architect Paul Wharton, who later would

Post Vandergriff

First council meeting with Mayor S.J. Stovall presiding. Mayor Stovall, City Attorney Tom Todd, and council members Carolyn Snider, Wayne Coble, Harold Patterson (19 January 1977).
—*Fort Worth Star-Telegram* Photograph Collection
Special Collections Division
The University of Texas at Arlington Libraries

also become a council member, invited S.J. Stovall to his home. He asked Stovall to run for a council position, which he did later that year. His opponent was Frank Wallace, a medical doctor. In his first council race, S.J. Stovall was defeated.

In 1963 at the urging of many of his fellow church members, including the pastor, Reverend Henard East, Stovall decided to run again. This time his opponent was an incumbent, Dixon Purvis, who owned a local downtown hardware store. This election cycle Stovall would be a winner and begin a two-decade service as a council member and mayor.

In the spring of 1963, in addition to Stovall's defeat of Dixon Purvis, another incumbent was defeated, which was unusual. Jack Crippen, an employee of LTV, defeated H.A.D. "Hoss" Dunsworth, who had served on the council for a decade.

Jack Crippen had the support of the local Jaycee chapter, which at the time was very active in Arlington politics. So active was the local Jaycee chapter that some established Arlington leaders were motivated to eventually establish an opposition group called "Young Men for Arlington."

The Jaycees at the time had many members who lived in Arlington but worked elsewhere. This perhaps gave them a degree of political independence they may not have had otherwise. These young professionals were in favor of a civil service system for fire and police personnel and opposed some projects and plans furthered by more establishment interests.[9]

After completing the remaining term as mayor after Vandergriff's resignation, Stovall ran successfully for three full terms. Most of his re-election attempts drew minor opposition, except in 1981 when challenged by Ken Groves. However, in his second successful re-election bid in 1979, the issue of single-member districts and civil service for some city employees was on the ballot as well.

It was a very intense and often bitter campaign, and voter turnout was especially heavy relative to past elections. Ken Groves, who later would run against S.J. Stovall for mayor, was instrumental in getting single-member districts and civil service on the ballot. Both of these propositions were opposed strongly by established city interests. And they were both defeated. (See Table 4.1.)

	APRIL 7, 1979				
	SINGLE MEMBER DISTRICTS		CIVIL SERVICE POLICEMEN & FIREMEN		
	FOR	AGAINST	FOR	AGAINST	TOTALS
B.M. POPE #3,217	447	768	396	824	1349
WIMBISH #26,55,228	586	990	482	1099	1723
LITTLE #28,29,30,173, 219,220,223	692	793	560	936	1594
BOWIE #7,27,31,174, 226,229	842	990	737	1110	1908
CENTRAL FIRE #52,161	342	442	334	465	843
CROW #100	166	206	156	215	412
BAILEY #112,147,205	356	965	333	1002	1443
BLANTON #143,168	352	506	320	542	927
FERGUSON #145,169,180, 210,225	709	483	608	595	1273
KOOKEN #148,158,190, 224	179	226	191	214	440
DUFF #171,181	476	956	510	920	1507
TOTALS	5147	7325	4627	7922	13,419

Table 4.1
Single Member District and Civil Service Election, 2 November 1993
City Secretary's Office

The single-member district issue was so divisive in the community that those in favor of the single-member district proposition claimed "dirty tricks" by the opponents of the measure. It was alleged that college students were hired by opponents to dress like "hippies" and hand out leaflets at voting locations on election day in favor of single-member districts. The idea was to make it appear that "a bunch of hippies" were in favor of the proposal and thus turn voters against it.

In 1979 Channel 8, WFAA-TV, televised an interview with a UTA student who admitted she had been hired to engage in similar "dirty trick" antics during the election.

The allegations were denied by the campaign, attributing such acts to unauthorized individuals (rogue elements) who had engaged in the unethical behavior.

In 1981 council member Ken Groves would resign his council seat to run against S.J. Stovall in what would be S.J. Stovall's toughest re-election bid. He defeated Groves. (See Table 4.2.) In 1983 he decided he would not run again for mayor.

Mayor Stovall's tenure as mayor was marked by the continuation of fast growth. However, attention of the city would now be directed to infrastructure as well. In the fall of 1977 city property taxes were raised for the first time and a large bond issue was proposed and passed. "Arlington's fast and continued growth got us out of potential financial troubles...."[10]

Mayor Stovall's tenure in office was characterized by some annexation of surrounding areas. Also, controversial and often very confrontational zoning cases marked his administration. Among the most prominent in the early 1980s was one labeled "Baird Farm," which was located in the northeast sector of the city. New concepts like condominiums and zero-lot line homes became common. The issue of new apartment construction permeated many of the zoning cases.

As a member of the council before becoming mayor, Stovall remembers several informal meetings of council members away from city hall relative to city items. These were held prior to the state Open Meetings Act. One such episode involved a hastily called conference in 1970 by Mayor Vandergriff in regard to the mayor pro-tempore, Charles Brown. Charles Brown had been a member of the council since 1963. He was known affectionately by his friends as "Charlie Brown," and was the owner of a lumber business. The informal meeting was held at a local motel on Division Street in Arlington, the Cibola Inn, to brief council members about the mayor pro-tempore's sudden disappearance. The council was told that the mayor pro-tempore had suddenly left the city. "He had parked his car, left his wife and business behind, and headed for California."[11]

Mayor S.J. Stovall's style and grasp of city politics was a perfect fit for the transition period after Mayor Vandergriff's

PRECINCT LOCATION AND NUMBER	MAYOR		
	GROVES	STOVALL	W.I.
BAILEY #181, 205	354	711	
BOWIE #7, 27, 30, 31, 226	485	624	
BUTLER #55, 228	423	851	Bryan 1
CARTER #52, 100, 161	361	525	
CONV. & VISITORS #148, 224	123	127	
DITTO #173, 220	409	602	
DUFF #112, 171	344	661	
FERGUSON #145, 210, 225	294	326	
GUNN #174, 229	253	482	
LITTLE #28, 29, 219	322	323	
NICHOLS #26, 190	258	398	
POPE #3, 217	335	808	
RANKIN #143, 169	188	330	
SOUTH DAVIS #147, 168	254	557	
YOUNG #223	168	202	
ABSENTEE VOTES	125	370	
TOTAL	4,696	7,899	1

Table 4.2
Groves-Stovall Mayoral Election, 4 April 1981
City Secretary's Office, Arlington, Texas

Mayor S. J. Stovall (22 November 1979).
—*Fort Worth Star-Telegram* Photograph Collection
Special Collections Division
The University of Texas at Arlington Libraries

long tenure in office. After deciding not to run again for mayor in 1983, Stovall was appointed to the Tarrant County Commissioners Court to fill the unexpired term of longtime and respected commissioner Jerry Mebus, who had died while holding a commissioner position.[12]

After finishing the unexpired term, S.J. Stovall then decided to hold his post as commissioner. He ran under the Democratic party label and was defeated by Republican O.L. Watson. This was the same year, 1984, that Tom Vandergriff, then a Democratic Congressman, was defeated in the Republican-Reagan landslide by Dick Armey. Representative Armey went on to eventually become the Republican majority leader in the House of Representatives in the 1990s.

After S.J. Stovall decided not to run again for mayor, another longtime council member decided to run for the position. Harold Patterson, a local banker for many years, had served on the council with S.J. Stovall during the Tom Vandergriff era. The policies and general direction of city politics would remain undisturbed.

Harold Patterson was born in Arlington near the present intersection of Highway 360 and Arkansas Lane. He attended Arlington High School, where his classmate was Tom Vandergriff. In the 1950s he had been in the banking business in Grand Prairie, but eventually moved his banking business to Arlington.

In 1966 he had become president of the Arlington National Bank. One council member at the time, M.D. "Buck" Buchanan, had decided not to run again. The entire city council and the mayor then came to Harold Patterson and asked him to consider running for that place on the council. He decided to run for the council and easily won his first election with only minor opposition.[13]

For all of his many terms on the council he usually faced minor opposition in his re-election bids. Perhaps his most serious opposition as a council member in an election was from Arlington resident, Jerry Pikulinski.

Harold Patterson's principal political theme was that of unity. And he credits much of Arlington's early successes to a lack of negative publicity that surrounded many other communities' politics during the same time period. "The business community (in Arlington), real estate, chamber of commerce, and even the churches...all worked together."[14]

As a council member perhaps the most volatile issue was whether the city should fluoridate the water supply. The issue of water fluoridation was also a matter of some debate in many other communities at the time. After a prolonged debate within the council and the community at large the city eventually decided in favor of fluoridation.

Harold Patterson became mayor in 1983. His main issue in his election bid was for increased funding for streets and thoroughfares. The money spent on these two endeavors nearly doubled during his two terms as mayor. His first bid for

Mayor Harold Patterson (15 March 1985).
—*Fort Worth Star-Telegram* Photograph Collection
Special Collections Division
The University of Texas at Arlington Libraries

mayor drew relatively minor opposition from a resident named Dan Leach. Mayor Patterson remembers it as "not a real tough race." [15]

However, in his second bid for re-election to the mayor's post he faced significant opposition from Gary Bruner, who was mayor pro-tempore at the time. Gary Bruner had served two terms on the council, elected in both 1981 and 1983. In 1985 he decided to run against Mayor Patterson.

There was much speculation about whether Mayor

Post Vandergriff 57

City Council work session. Council member Gary Bruner, center left, with folder in hand, is seated next to Mayor Patterson, center.

—*Fort Worth Star-Telegram* Photograph Collection
Special Collections Division
The University of Texas at Arlington Libraries

Patterson would draw a significant opponent in his re-election bid. When Gary Bruner emerged as the principal challenger many pundits believed it would be a very close race. The outcome, however, was in Mayor Patterson's favor, beating the challenger by sixty to forty percent.

Gary Bruner's main challenge to Harold Patterson pivoted on the mayor's leadership style and direction. He argued that the mayor had not brought enough new business to the community.

However, Mayor Patterson's long tenure on the council and the political ties that he had helped forge for many years helped in his handy defeat of the erstwhile challenger.

Under Harold Patterson's tenure as mayor, the city's bond rating increased. Mayor Patterson also took great pride that during his administration he was able to turn back "attempts by the city staff to transfer money from the water and sewer account into the general revenue fund." [16]

In 1987 he decided he would not make another re-election attempt as mayor. He left the council having compiled one of the longest tenures as a council member and mayor. Mayor Patterson was an important link in the continuity that bound the city's elites together for nearly half a century.

Richard Greene, who succeeded Harold Patterson as mayor in 1987, believed that Arlington was indeed the best place in the world to live. To some that may sound a bit overstated, yet if you are going to be a good and vibrant mayor you had better believe it. And he did!

Richard Greene, intense and determined, was clearly in control of any undertaking. He was a good speaker at any event and could read from a prepared script or extemporize equally as well. Like Tom Vandergriff he seemed to relish the opportunity to speak before groups and tailored his remarks to fit the audience.

He arrived in Arlington in 1967 from Louisiana as a loan officer with a First Fidelity Mortgage Company seeking a base in an expanding city. Upon his arrival, he wrote Mayor Tom Vandergriff informing him about his loan business. Mayor Vandergriff responded with a handwritten note welcoming him to the city. It would be the beginning of a deep

Richard Greene.
—*Fort Worth Star-Telegram* Photograph Collection
Special Collections Division
The University of Texas at Arlington Libraries

and important political and economic alliance between these two men.

In that year, 1967, he became active in a variety of civic groups. At the time, he understood that civic involvement was one way to expand both economic and political interests. Before coming to Arlington, he had been a member of a Lions Club in Louisiana.

Early on, Richard Greene became successful and established a favorable reputation as a loan officer. He also had been told that aside from Tom Vandergriff the other person to know would be Howard Wilemon of the Arlington State Bank. In 1969 he was brought into Arlington Savings as a vice-president, and eventually, at the age of twenty-seven, he became president of Arlington Savings.

He then set about arranging a local group of investors to purchase Arlington Savings from a Houston financial organization. Eventually Arlington Savings would be sold to Sunbelt Savings in 1984 and Richard Greene became president of the Arlington Division of Sunbelt Savings.

Later he would leave Sunbelt and form his own mortgage company, Savings Banc, located in Arlington. In 1989 he learned that Tom Vandergriff was interested in selling his Chevrolet dealership, so with another group of investors he purchased the dealership. He and other investors would purchase yet another dealership, McDavid Acura, and rename it Vandergriff Acura.

However, in a short while the Vandergriff Chevrolet and Acura dealerships would be sold to out-of-state investors and he would leave the automobile business entirely. After deciding not to run again for mayor in 1997, he joined the *Arlington Star-Telegram* as head of community relations and later as an assistant publisher. In 2000 he would assume an executive position with the North Texas Olympic Committee striving to bring the 2012 Olympics to the area.

His abilities and expertise in the financial world would serve him well in the political arena as well. He would be looked upon for leadership in both fields. And his reputation as a political leader would often be compared to that of Tom Vandergriff.

Mayors Vandergriff, Stovall, Patterson, and Greene were all able to order up just the right ingredients from the political menu. Each had special talents which fit the problems and mood of the moment: Tom Vandergriff, who had grand ideas for a small town and saw them through to fruition; S.J. Stovall and Harold Patterson, who solidified the gains and cared for the infrastructure after years of tumultuous growth; and Richard Greene, who would infuse the city with a new burst of energy and projects.

Richard Greene was mayor for ten years, from 1987 to 1997. But it is likely that if he so wished, he might have been able to match the political longevity of Tom Vandergriff.

Richard Greene always was interested in city politics. It was pertinent to his business as an executive with a large mortgage company. Land traditionally had been the basis for wealth and power in this community. Mortgage companies, like real estate offices, have a vested interest in seeing a city grow and prosper both commercially and with new residences.

In 1975 Greene's more formal career in city government was launched. Mayor Tom Vandergriff appointed him to the prestigious Planning and Zoning Commission. He would remain on the Planning and Zoning Commission, referred to by politicos as "P and Z," for nine years.

In 1978, however, he decided to run for a position on the city council. His principal opponent was Kenneth Groves, a longtime resident, architect, engineer, and surveyor. Ken Groves, like Richard Greene, had a keen interest in city politics for many years. Kenneth Groves, however, did not have a base in the establishment at the time. His candidacy was viewed as that of an upstart, a maverick, who had little chance against the establishment figure, Richard Greene.

Some of Ken Groves' support came from community activists who had for many years not agreed with the direction of the city. Betty and Nile Fischer, Dr. Elliot Blumberg, and Kay Taebel, who would later become a council member, were principal supporters of Ken Groves.

He was able to tap into a lingering discontent. He would support single-member districts, increased restrictions on residential and commercial developments, and inclusion of a more diverse group of people on city boards and commissions. He would generally oppose what he referred to as "the good ole' boy system."

Among the politically active in the community, it was broadly assumed that Richard Greene would win the council spot handily. He ran a very traditional campaign, similar to that which propelled most establishment-based candidates to victories. This meant having paid political ads in local newspapers and mobilizing the civic and service club membership to back his candidacy.

Ken Groves ran a very untraditional campaign for the city

council. He was very alert to the way statewide and national campaigns had been run and applied that to local politics.

He engaged in "target mailing," which meant specific mail-outs to special constituencies. He would target the problems in a specific neighborhood and aim the campaign letter to them. He walked door-to-door in some neighborhoods talking about their indigenous problems, whatever they might be.

The Groves-Greene campaign was a very intense race between two skilled politicians. The day of the election, the political supporters for Richard Greene were very comfortable, some might say even a bit overconfident of victory. How could Richard Greene lose? And yet, he did lose! (See Table 4.3 for election results.) To Richard Greene, the "loss to Groves was devastating." [17]

The loss of the council race to Ken Groves had a galvanizing effect on Richard Greene. Early on he relied on advice and alliances from the traditional establishment community. However, after the loss to Ken Groves he began to broaden his base of support and reach out more to diverse interests, though not abandoning his old base.

He would meet, if the occasion arose, with those who had backed Ken Groves. Indeed he may have had an increased respect for those community interests whose agenda was different from those usually articulated by city leaders.

His reaching out to a more broad-based constituency would serve him well later on when he would once again contend for a city council position and later as mayor. Interestingly, in 1984, six years after he had lost a bruising election to Ken Groves, it would be Groves who would reach out to Richard Greene and ask him to run for a council seat.

In 1984 Richard Greene won handily against Richard Marcotte. From this point on, his political life would rise rapidly. In 1985, after only a brief time on the council, he was elected mayor pro-tempore. In 1986 he would run and win his council seat again. In 1987, with Mayor Harold Patterson deciding not to run again, Richard Greene resigned his council seat and prepared to run for mayor.

However, one other prominent council member had a wish to become mayor as well. Dottie Lynn, a longtime resident of

Post Vandergriff 63

PRECINCT LOCATION AND NUMBER	CITY ELECTION - APRIL 1, 1978							
	PLACE 4					PLACE 5	
	PENNINGTON	GROVES	GREENE	LITZ	W.I.	WALKER	W.I.
B. M. POPE #3, 217	10	221	194	6		340	2
WIMBISH #26, 55, 228	12	280	185	11		383	
LITTLE #28, 29, 30, 173, 219, 220, 223	19	231	176	22		336	
BOWIE #7, 27, 31, 174, 226, 229	12	242	252	6		406	6
CENTRAL FIRE #52, 161	8	192	117	10		250	
CROW #100	8	89	47	2		112	1
BAILEY #112, 147, 205	8	219	325	11		460	5
BLANTON #143, 168	13	175	126	1		243	2
FERGUSON #145; 169, 180, 210, 225	31	177	105	9		258	
KOOKEN #148, 158, 190, 224	6	85	38	3		106	
DUFF #171, 181	20	251	270	7		454	5
TOTALS	147	2162	1835	88		3348	15

Table 4.3
Groves-Greene City Council Election, 1 April 1978
City Secretary's Office, Arlington, Texas

Arlington and another Tom Vandergriff appointee to the Planning and Zoning Commission, decided to run. She, like Richard Greene, also resigned from the council to make the race.

The 1987 campaign for mayor was perhaps the most bruising mayoral contest since the Stovall-Groves race nearly a decade earlier. Dottie Lynn had a large group of friends loyal to her since she first was elected to the council in 1982. Jo Johnston, a good friend and prominent real estate executive, was treasurer of Lynn's campaign.

Richard Greene (8 November 1984).
—*Fort Worth Star-Telegram* Photograph Collection
Special Collections Division
The University of Texas at Arlington Libraries

Lynn's campaign was built around a theme of her being a "people person." She relied on past support, like "Church Women United," which had helped elect her to the council. She reminisces that "It was a very intense race, often bitter at times." [18]

Two former mayors, Vandergriff and Stovall, supported Richard Greene, while former mayor Harold Patterson remained neutral.[19] Tom Vandergriff's support of Richard Greene was very public, which was noteworthy due to his usual unwillingness to publicly endorse candidates.

Though this mayor's race was very heated at times, there was hardly any doubt that Richard Greene would win. And in the final outcome he won handily. His base of support in the community was now much greater than at any time he had entered city politics. His name was well recognized throughout the community and he had solid establishment support. Further, he had learned political lessons from his only political defeat in the earlier council election against Ken Groves. His mayoral campaign would be much more sophisticated than his earlier races, evidenced by his hiring of an important political consultant, Bryan Eppstein of Fort Worth.

Richard Greene spent about $80,000 and Dottie Lynn about $50,000. The cost of mounting a serious citywide campaign had become very expensive. In relative terms, this campaign in the year 2001 may have totaled $150,000 for Greene and $120,000 for Lynn. And future campaigns for citywide political offices would match these amounts.

Richard Greene's service as mayor would last a full decade. And within that decade he would be faced with major challenges and opportunities comparable in ways to the Vandergriff era.

Richard Greene was aware, upon assuming office, that the two main citizen concerns were traffic and crime. Prior to his taking office and throughout his tenure, the budget of the police and fire departments almost doubled in size. Also, more money for streets and thoroughfares was allocated through the passage of bond issues.

And always, as in past mayoral administrations, there was the tension of trying to hold taxes at current levels and maintain or increase the level of services.

Several challenges to the city and for Greene as mayor were presented in 1991. The General Motors plant, which had always been the important economic signature for Arlington, was threatened with closure. General Motors was to decide whether to close its Arlington plant or a similar plant in Michigan.

Mayor Greene rallied the entire city behind the GM plant. According to Mayor Greene, it had to remain open. Arlington would not be the same without it. Bumper stickers, rallies, and a number of statewide political officials joined the economic chorus of keeping the plant in Arlington open. Democratic Congressman Martin Frost, Republican Congressman Dick

Armey, and Governor Ann Richards were representative of the many who gave support to Arlington and GM remaining together. Also, organized labor at the Arlington location gave its support to the GM plant in Arlington.

Finally, after much tension and speculation about which plant GM would choose to keep open, a decision was reached. The Arlington plant would remain open and some Michigan plant employees could, if they wished, be transferred to Arlington. It was an important challenge to Mayor Greene. He had preserved the legacy left to him by Tom Vandergriff.

In the same year, 1991, voters in Arlington approved an increase in the sales tax to construct a new baseball stadium for the Texas Rangers. Like the General Motors Corporation, the baseball club, which had played in Arlington for many years, was speculating about moving to another place. They wanted a bigger, more modern stadium with luxury boxes.

Dallas, Texas, had lost the Dallas Cowboys football team to Irving, Texas, in prior years although it retained the Dallas name. The professional football team had been playing at the Cotton Bowl and wanted a more modern state-of-the art field. Irving, Texas, lured the team away from Dallas when Dallas leaders could not or would not provide what the team desired.

Now, some Dallas leaders and sports columnists were speculating about Dallas luring the Texas Rangers baseball team. The downtown area of Dallas was talked about as the most likely place for the Texas Rangers if they moved from Arlington. Other towns in the area were also discussing the possibility of joining the bidding war to attract the Texas Rangers.

The Texas Rangers decided to remain in Arlington. The city agreed to put a referendum before voters to build the Rangers a new stadium. The major question was whether the citizens of Arlington would help pay for it with a half-cent sales tax. The answer was a clear "yes." And in 1991, after a massive campaign to mobilize Arlington voters to vote for the sales tax increase, it passed overwhelmingly. The campaign was so successful it brought out one of the largest voter turnouts ever for a non-presidential year. (See Table 4.4.)

Post Vandergriff

PRECINCTS	TOTAL VOTES	PROPOSITION NO. 1 (Sales Tax Increase)	
		For	Against
ANDERSON	1021	660	361
ATHERTON	1132	697	435
BAILEY	1598	996	602
BERRY	1149	664	485
BLANTON	908	462	446
BOLES	2101	1362	739
COREY	1140	718	422
DITTO	1445	875	570
DUFF	1356	914	442
ELLIS	1169	939	230
FIRE PREVENTION	547	306	241
FITZGERALD	1263	827	436
GUNN	1472	909	563
MILLER	1380	913	467
MORTON	1096	605	491
POPE	1417	1014	403
SHACKELFORD	1136	870	266
SHERROD	1656	1277	379
SO. DAVIS	776	430	346
THORNTON	706	360	346
WIMBISH	1169	737	432
YOUNG	2032	1357	675
ABSENTEE	6191	4032	2159
TOTAL	33860	21924	11936

CITY OF ARLINGTON SPECIAL ELECTION
JANUARY 19, 1991

Table 4.4
Ball Park Sales Tax Election
City Secretary's Office, Arlington, Texas

Mayor Greene worked tirelessly for the Ballpark sales tax proposal. Drawings of the proposed stadium were publicized, its location specified, and the numerous benefits accruing from its construction were identified.

The sales tax proposal was not without its opponents, however. There were those who opposed the sales tax proposal arguing that a public entity should not subsidize a private corporation. Others raised repeated questions about the economic benefits to Arlington and the proposed terms of the contract with the Texas Rangers.

But Mayor Richard Greene had once again been able to keep intact and indeed expand one of the principal legacies of the Vandergriff era. The professional baseball team, lured away from Washington, D.C. years before, would remain in Arlington and play ball in an expanded and architecturally significant ballpark.

When Richard Greene became mayor, he was also faced with the prospects of an economic downturn and city budget problems. The economy of the entire state in the mid-to-late 1980s was suffering from a dramatic downturn in oil prices and a crumbling of its old economy. Near the end of his five full terms as mayor, he could boast of more jobs and billions of dollars in new capital investments by corporations like National Semiconductor, Doskocil Manufacturing, General Motors, and Hughes Corporation.

Richard Greene as mayor was a consensus builder. He was able to mobilize at least a majority of the council on most issues and all of them on important items like the Ballpark. He admits that there were very frustrating times as well.

Council members who had their own agendas were, he believed, counterproductive to his perspective of the city's overall interest. This was also true of some neighborhood groups. One incident illustrates the frustration. One neighborhood group strongly opposed a section of Green Oaks Boulevard, which was designed to encircle the city. Their opposition was eventually overcome.

Richard Greene became noted for tagging people who were against major city projects as "naysayers." He understood, though differed with, those who were philosophically opposed to the Ballpark sales tax proposal. Many people simply opposed the idea of subsidizing millionaire sports team owners. But the labeling of "naysayers" largely applied to those who seemed to be opposed to any city project.

The era in which Richard Greene served as mayor was different from the Vandergriff period. The city was now much bigger in land area and population. And the city was fundamentally different in the degree of diversity.

At the end of regular Tuesday council meetings, a period was set aside for citizens to voice any complaint, ask any question, or simply address the council and mayor. The number of citizens participating in this opportunity noticeably increased in the early 1980s and continued to increase in pace during much of Richard Greene's tenure.

Dottie Lynn, who served on the council for eighteen years, stated, "People have higher expectations now. Back when I started, there wasn't much citizen participation. Now we have a lot of people coming to the council meetings, and that's helped the governance of the city. These people have come from other places, bringing new ideas to the city." [20]

Though at times frustrated, Richard Greene, like the mayors before him, genuinely liked being mayor. Public appearances, meeting mayors of other cities, greeting foreign visitors energized him. As mayor he was a forceful advocate for his agenda items. He encouraged citizens to be council candidates or apply for membership on city boards and commissions. However, there was never the intense recruitment of candidates as in the past.

Richard Greene has often been compared to Tom Vandergriff. And the similarities are apparent. Both men enjoyed the public arena. Both were excellent speakers. Both mayors sought unanimity and consensus. Both set their sights on growth and significance for Arlington. "Arlington is nobody's suburb!" became Richard Greene's proud rejoinder to those who perceived Arlington as a minor player in the region.

Richard Greene worked to cement the legacy of Tom Vandergriff. The Texas Rangers remained in Arlington and, following the successful sales tax election, played in a state-of-the-art sports facility. The General Motors plant remained open and even expanded.

Like Tom Vandergriff before him, Greene would answer his telephone calls personally and return calls promptly. He would add the "personal touch" to his political position. He served five consecutive terms as mayor. However, if he so wished, Greene most likely could have matched Tom Vandergriff's twenty-six-year time span in the mayor's office.

Unlike Tom Vandergriff, however, he was not called upon on an almost daily basis for special favors and demands. Though considered a powerful and forceful leader, the city of Arlington was never "his" city as it once was under the leadership of Tom Vandergriff. Mayor Vandergriff turned a small town into a city; Richard Greene gave it personality.

Chapter Five

Winners, Losers, Movers, Shakers: Shaping City Politics

Betty and Nile Fischer

Betty and Nile Fischer moved to Arlington in March 1957. Nile Fischer was an engineer with one of the many defense firms in the area. Betty Fischer was a political activist, especially within the Democratic Party. Later in her political career she was elected as head of the Tarrant County Democratic Party. The couple has always been referred to by their many political acquaintances as simply "Betty and Nile."

Quite early after moving to their new home in east Arlington they experienced some water drainage problems on their property. They sought a solution and quickly found out that Mayor Tom Vandergriff was the key to "making things happen."[1]

Betty Fischer's political philosophy had been shaped by her continuing involvement in the Democratic Party, especially the liberal wing of the party. She took an especially active role in the campaigns of politicians like Don Gladden of Fort Worth in his election bid for the Texas House of Representatives and his sub-

Betty Fischer, Civic Activist (21 March 1979).
—*Fort Worth Star-Telegram* Photograph Collection
Special Collections Division
The University of Texas at Arlington Libraries

sequent but losing effort to become the state's lieutenant governor. She supported and actively campaigned for State Senator Don Kennard of Fort Worth, Democratic Congressman Martin Frost, and United States Senator Ralph Yarborough.

She is proud of her liberalism and has maintained this political perspective for all of her adult life. Nile Fischer, her husband, likewise shared her political philosophy, but because of his job commitments did not maintain as high a political profile as wife Betty.

Betty Fischer always was intense, focused, and clearly determined. She would be fiercely loyal to someone as long as they continued to represent the politics she held important. Otherwise, she would let them know of her displeasure.

Later, she and her husband Nile moved to a home in central Arlington where she would hold "court" for many political discussion groups, candidates, and city and state officeholders. If a city council election or issue was on the ballot that she thought important, her small home would be filled with campaign literature ready to be mailed.

Potential candidates for city office would often seek her counsel and support, especially those who knew that they would not receive local elite help. She played a role starting in the early 1960s and for several decades later, "driving the good ole' boys crazy!" according to Ken Groves, a council member who received her support.[2]

Betty Fischer's overall political philosophy was quickly adapted to many local issues and political personalities in Arlington. Equality of representation, distribution of power, and lessening of taxation on poorer population groups became her goals.

She believed that the city was overlooking basic infrastructure needs like streets, thoroughfares, and libraries. She held that the city was placing too much emphasis on growth and not enough on what she called "quality of life" issues and "taking care of what is already here."[3]

To Betty Fischer, politics was all about ideas and opinions. The political candidate was not nearly so important as the ideas and issues proposed. Backing a candidate was important, but only based on the ideas represented.

In the 1960s local politics drew her attention. The issue of whether or not to fluoridate the city's drinking water became heated. Some groups believed that water fluoridation was a "communist plot." Betty Fischer sided with the pro-fluoride group, which eventually won in a non-binding city referendum. The city's water supply was eventually fluoridated.

In 1963 she was active in the campaign of Jack Crippen, an employee of LTV (Ling Temco Vought Corporation) who was elected to the city council. Crippen had as issues a civil service system for city police and fire personnel. Jack Crippen's campaign also pivoted on what he considered to be a diversion of bond money from a recent library bond election to other projects.[4]

She became allied at least at the issues level with the local Jaycee chapter. The Jaycees, in the early 1960s, were very active in local politics and supported a civil service system for police and fire personnel. The Jaycees also campaigned for and achieved an alteration in the way Arlington city council members were elected. Until 1960 there was no "place" system for council member designation.

Candidates from 1921 until 1960 would simply campaign to be an Arlington city "commissioner" as it was then called. The two candidates with the most votes would become commissioners. The mayor was elected at large in alternate years. During this period there were four commissioners and a mayor with staggered commissioner terms.

This was changed with Jaycee support to a "place" system. Candidates would now campaign for a specific place within the council. This system remained in effect until 1994.[5]

But the first major local political campaign, which galvanized the Fischers, was in 1967, when Arlington residents were to vote on a one percent sales tax. At that time, state law gave municipalities the option of adding a one percent sales tax, which after collection by the state would be remitted back to the city.

City leaders grabbed at the opportunity to add the one percent sales tax. It would be a way to keep property tax rates stable (though property valuations were increasing) and still meet service demands. Betty and Nile Fischer put their overall ideology to practical work in opposition.

They believed that a sales tax was a very regressive form of raising revenue. They organized a strong campaign to defeat the citywide referendum. Sam Hamlett, later to be a city council member, Jerry Jaggers, a three-time candidate for council, Duane Martin, a professor at the University of Texas at Arlington, Ralph Estes, an accounting professor also at the university, and then state senator Oscar Mauzy, all pitched in with the Fischers to defeat the measure.

The one percent city sales tax went down to defeat in a very heated and intense election. The Fischers mounted a targeted mail-out to designated Arlington households against the sales tax proposal. The election brought out a sizable number

RESOLUTION NO. 2950

RESOLUTION AND ORDER CANVASSING RETURNS AND DECLARING RESULTS OF SPECIAL ELECTION HELD IN THE CITY OF ARLINGTON, TEXAS, ON DECEMBER 5, 1967, ON THE QUESTION OF ADOPTION OF A ONE PER CENT (1%) LOCAL SALES AND USE TAX WITHIN SAID CITY.

WHEREAS, there was held in the City of Arlington, Texas, on the 5th day of December, 1967, an election at which there were submitted to the duly qualified resident electors of said City, for their action thereupon, the following propositions:

FOR adoption of a one per cent (1%) local sales and use tax within the city.

AGAINST adoption of a one per cent (1%) local sales and use tax within the city.

and

WHEREAS, there were cast at said election __4,347__ votes, of which number there were cast:

FOR addoption of a one per cent (1%) local sales and use tax within the city __2,154__ votes

AGAINST adoption of a one per cent (1%) local sales and use tax within the city __2,193__ votes

Majority AGAINST adoption of a one per cent (1%) local sales and use tax within the city __39__ votes

as shown in the official election returns heretofore lawfully submitted to the City Council of the City of Arlington, Texas, and filed with the City Secretary of said City; and

WHEREAS, only duly qualified resident electors of said City voted at said election, and said election was called and held in strict conformity with the laws of the State of Texas; NOW THEREFORE BE IT RESOLVED AND ORDERED BY THE CITY COUNCIL OF THE CITY OF ARLINGTON, TEXAS:

Table 5.1
Defeat of One Cent Local Sales Tax by 39 Votes
City Secretary's Office, Arlington, Texas

of voters relative to past elections. The sales tax was defeated by thirty-nine votes. (See Table 5.1.)

At a later date in 1969 the one percent city sales tax was put before a citywide vote again. Before this second tax election Betty Fischer appeared at a meeting of the city council. She spoke about what she perceived to be unfair campaigning by proponents. Mayor Vandergriff reprimanded her by saying that she had cost the city millions of dollars in lost tax revenue from the previous failed sales tax election. Quite the contrary, she replied, "I saved Arlington citizens millions of dollars!"[6]

This time, however, the sales tax passed. And it passed by a rather large margin of 2,628 votes. This was a remarkable turnaround from the earlier defeat. Many other municipalities were adding the sales tax to their coffers as well through elections.

Betty Fischer was now fully immersed in Arlington city politics. In three consecutive election cycles she supported candidates for city council. In 1964, 1966, and 1968 she strongly supported Jerry Jaggers for city council. Jaggers shared her basic philosophy of governance.

All three campaigns by Jaggers were against a local attorney, John Ball. And in all three attempts against councilman Ball, Jaggers was defeated. However, it was a very close and hard fought contest in all three campaigns. Again, the Jaycees played an important role in city politics by supporting Jaggers against John Ball.

Due to the Jaycees' continued support for what could be labeled anti-establishment views, a new organization, the "Young Men for Arlington," was organized to support more establishment directions and candidates.

In 1971, Betty Fischer decided to run for a council place. A council seat was open, meaning no incumbent was running, and she placed her name on the ballot. Her principal opponent was Dr. R.G. "Wick" Alexander, a prominent orthodontist in the city.

It would not be surprising that many local elites would frown on her candidacy. The Arlington *Citizen-Journal* editorialized against her. She knew she would be in a tough election fight.

There were multiple candidates vying for the open position. She and Dr. Alexander were close in vote totals, but he

Carolyn Snider (22 March 1979).
—Courtesy of family of Carolyn Snider

was the leading candidate. There was at the time no provision for a run-off election. So Dr. Alexander was declared the victor and remained on the council for three full consecutive terms.

Until Betty Fischer's candidacy in 1971, no woman had ever run a highly competitive campaign for city council. Though she lost the election she helped pave the way for other women who would eventually run for city office and win.

Betty Fischer continued her support for candidates and issues she identified with. In 1975 she supported Allan Saxe against Carolyn W. Snider. Carolyn Snider was perhaps one of Arlington's most well-known and prominent citizens, who could trace family roots back to the early days of the city.

Her husband, Dr. Richard Snider, had been a member of

the city council years earlier. And her son, Bill Snider, would become a council member serving multiple terms in the 1980s.

In 1975 there was an open seat on the council, Place 1, which had previously been held by Doland C. Maner, an executive with Southern Industrial Steel Company, who decided not to seek re-election.

Six candidates contested for the open position. Allan Saxe and Carolyn Snider were the top two in vote totals and a run-off election was scheduled. Both in the general and the run-off elections, Betty Fischer worked for Saxe with mail-outs, yard signs, and fundraisers.

At the time Saxe was viewed as the anti-establishment candidate and drew support from a variety of groups and individuals at odds with the city establishment. Carolyn Snider drew support from the traditional banking, real estate, chamber of commerce, and city leaders.

The race was very colorful and even fun-filled, which did not fit the description of most council races. Many college students, not in Saxe's Political Science classes, participated. They designed campaign T-shirts, colorful handouts, and walked door-to-door campaigning for Saxe. "Arlington Needs Saxe" bumper stickers (see photo next page) were seen about town with the letter "e" positioned over the letter "a" in Saxe's name, changing the slogan to "Arlington Needs Sex." The campaign (in part) and voter registration efforts were directed at those citizens not usually prone to register.

In many of Arlington's council elections in the 1960s to 1970s, it became a tradition to hand out campaign literature for various candidates at Arlington's banks. Candidates and their supporters, as the election date drew near, would deliver pamphlets to cars waiting in drive-through lines or those patrons entering the banks on foot. Very often this became a festive event for all, bringing many in the community into the political process. In the Saxe-Snider election this was done several times prior to the general election and the run-off as well.

In the run-off election, a unique event was held at the Arlington Community Center. The League of Women Voters sponsored a non-traditional, two-candidate run-off debate. The debate pivoted upon an informal question-and-answer

Arlington NEEDS SAXE

PAID FOR BY ALLAN SAXE, 2209 WESTWOOD ARLINGTON, TEXAS 76012
PRINTED BY ELMER INGLE, 1632 PARK PLACE, FT. WORTH 76110

format. The community center was filled to capacity as the two candidates debated and fielded audience questions.

In the run-off, Carolyn Snider narrowly defeated Allan Saxe. Carolyn Snider went on to distinguish herself on the council until her untimely death on June 17, 1982.

Betty Fischer continued her work for council candidates. In 1977 she helped Sam Hamlett in his successful campaign for a council seat. In 1978 she assisted Ken Groves in his upset victory over Richard Greene for a council position.

In addition to helping on campaigns she worked for single-member districts and a broader representation on city boards and commissions. After her own council defeat she appeared before the city council and asked to be appointed to the Planning and Zoning Commission. Her request was denied.

Betty and Nile Fischer viewed power to be influenced to a large extent by economic considerations. Until 1979 property valuation for tax purposes was done solely by local governmental entities throughout the state. Interestingly, for some time property tax collection was managed by the city both for the school system as well as the city.

The Fischers viewed this powerful tool of appraising property for taxes and collecting them as part of the power structure of governmental entities. With each governmental entity (school, city, county, and others) having different valuation for the same piece of property, it made the system often bewildering and unfair.

However, by 1979 the state legislature of Texas ended this practice of separate valuation of property. It was formally titled the Texas Property Tax Code of 1979. Labeled by the media after its principal author, the Peveto Bill provided for a single appraisal district in each county.

All taxing entities were now to use the same appraised value for any given piece of property, and all property was to be appraised at 100% of fair market value. Counties would now be responsible under state law for the appraisal and taxing authority, which formerly rested with a variety of local governmental units. The Tarrant Appraisal District, which included Arlington in its jurisdiction, was thus formally created.

What this meant for Arlington is that valuation of property for schools and the city would be done by this new entity called the Tarrant Appraisal District (TAD). The Fischers believed that this once powerful taxing and appraisal lever of local government had been taken from cities.

Betty and Nile Fischer played an important role in the city's politics, especially the two decades of the 1960s and 1970s. They were simultaneously critics, political observers, and bold activists.

Barton Thompson versus Martha Walker
And
Ralph Shelton versus Paul Yarbrough

For many years the establishment, consisting of groups of local elites, shared the same basic goals. If there were differences among them, and there were, they never surfaced for public viewing.

Mayor Tom Vandergriff would support those council members who wished to be re-elected. He was very loyal and supportive of his council. If vacancies occurred, the mayor and council would recruit citizens to fill various posts.

Mayor Vandergriff, however, never relished endorsing any candidate who was not already on the council. Traditionally, he would be very non-committal publicly. The year 1972 saw two important breaks in the traditional operation of city politics. Mayor Vandergriff would openly endorse a non-incumbent in a highly competitive race and not give his support, or at least not campaign actively, for an incumbent up for re-election.

In 1972 two heated city council elections spilled over and affected each campaign. Both campaigns revealed, perhaps for the first time, splits within the elite structure of the community. One contest featured an incumbent, Barton Thompson, who had been elected in 1970 to a vacant place previously held by John Ball. The mayor and council supported his candidacy at the time.

Barton Thompson came to Arlington in 1946 although he had earlier visited his grandparents who lived in the town as early as 1939. His father, Clarence Thompson, had served earlier on the Planning and Zoning Commission. Barton Thompson was an investor and developer.

In 1970 his support came from among others, James "Big Daddy" Knapp. James Knapp was a large landowner in Arlington and throughout Tarrant County. He also hosted the Arlington Bar Association on his farm in the adjacent Arlington community of Rendon in an annual late summer political event.

The Arlington Bar Association social invited state judges, local and state politicians, and other community notables and clients and friends of Arlington lawyers. It was a place to meet candidates, campaign, and engage in political gossip. James "Big Daddy" Knapp continued for many years to be a major supporter of selected Arlington candidates for office. Other principal supporters in Barton Thompson's candidacy were James Martin, Superintendent of the Arlington Independent School District, Howard Wilemon, of Arlington State Bank, and George Hawkes, publisher of the Arlington *Citizen-Journal*. Martha Hughes and Charles Merrill, longtime residents and friends, were his campaign managers.

In 1972 he ran for re-election and this time some of the traditional incumbent support that would usually come from the mayor's office did not seem to materialize. Barton Thompson's father, Clarence Thompson, had given his support to Paul Yarbrough, who was in a bruising political battle the same year against Ralph Shelton. Shelton had the strong support of the mayor and many establishment interests.

The race between Shelton and Yarbrough split the Arlington political, economic, and social establishment like no other before. The support of Yarbrough by Barton Thompson's father most likely contributed to the mayor and his political following moving away from Thompson.

Though some support that may have gone to Barton Thompson vanished, his opponent was formidable in her own right. Martha Walker was a longtime Arlington resident whose main base of support initially came from Church Women United, Saint Maria Goretti Catholic Church, and various other women's groups. She had arrived in Arlington in 1960 with her husband, who at the time had acquired a position in the Arlington State College Business School.

Martha Walker had sought Mayor Vandergriff's support in her council race, but he was, as usual, non-committal if an incumbent was up for re-election. The contest between Walker and Thompson was close, but not nearly as intense or bitter as the Shelton and Yarbrough race would be.

In the 1970s, the usual political pattern was for incumbents to run unopposed or to have very minor opposition. This time it would be different. Barton Thompson, the incumbent, would lose to the challenger, Martha Walker, in a close run-off election.

Martha Walker would become the first woman elected to serve on the city council. The year 1972 was an interesting one politically for women in Texas.

Frances "Sissy" Farenthold in the same year would make a strong showing in the Democratic primary for governor against a strong male opponent, Dolph Briscoe. Briscoe won the primary and went on to become governor of the state, but not before Farenthold had nearly upset the "good ole' boy" apparatus that had held the state politically for so many years.

Barton Thompson left the council without any acrimony and remained active in the community for many years. Even though he had only a brief tenure on the council, he and his family have resided in Arlington for years and have engaged in a variety of industrial and residential developments.

Thompson delights in retelling stories of old Arlington politics. In the 1950s, an Arlington city attorney was at a party in Fort Worth. There, a Fort Worth council member inadvertently mentioned that Fort Worth had intentions of quickly annexing part of what is now west Arlington—then unincorporated land.

If Fort Worth's rapid annexation plans had materialized,

Winners, Losers, Movers, Shakers: Shaping City Politics 83

Martha Walker (22 November 1979).
—*Fort Worth Star-Telegram* Photograph Collection
Special Collections Division
The University of Texas at Arlington Libraries

the city of Fort Worth would have been close to what is now Bowen Road. The city attorney, however, realizing the importance of what he had overheard, headed quickly back to Arlington, where the mayor convened a midnight session to annex the coveted land to Arlington.[7]

In later years, after the passage of the Open Meetings Act, no such quick meeting of the Arlington City Council could have been convened. And most likely the intentions of Fort Worth would have been known much earlier under today's state records and meetings laws than simply discovering them accidentally from an indiscreet Fort Worth council member.

Thompson remembers the early development of the

Seven Seas Amusement Park and its eventual demise. The land was first purchased by the city from Curtis Mathes, namesake of the famed television set manufacturer.

The Seven Seas theme park was originally to be operated by a contract with the Great Southwest Corporation, which was to manage the park. Barton Thompson had been sales manager of the Great Southwest Corporation.

The Pennsylvania Railroad owned stock in Great Southwest and the railroad was having a severe economic downturn, which affected Great Southwest. Great Southwest could no longer obtain a bond on its contract with the city. The city had the choice of contracting with other sea life developers like San Diego Sea Life or managing the park itself.

The city opted to build and run Seven Seas, which eventually failed. It was then leased for a brief time as another theme park named Hawaii Kai. The entire project was abandoned and the Arlington Convention Center presently stands on some of the land.[8]

Martha Walker's campaign against Barton Thompson included door-to-door electioneering. Her campaign was built around neighborhood coffees arranged by many of her friends developed in church organizations. After her election as the first woman to serve on the city council she had a long tenure of five consecutive terms (ten years) on the council. She would run repeatedly for re-election on a slate with Mayor Vandergriff's support.[9]

Her popularity and influence on the council was at times so strong that she thought about running for mayor. This was especially true after Mayor S.J. Stovall vacated the office in 1983. Most likely she would have run against Harold Patterson in the subsequent mayoral campaign. However, she left the council and the possibility of being mayor behind her. Her personal life and business required her full attention.[10]

Martha Walker's ten years on the council were busy times for council work. The 1970s was a boom period of development for Arlington. Zoning of property took up the majority of the council's agenda. Often there would be as many as seven or eight zoning cases a night.

Much of the land was still zoned agricultural and every

piece of land to be developed had to be re-zoned. It was not unusual for the council to meet long hours into the evening hearing zoning cases. In the 1970s many multi-family housing units (apartments) were zoned.

In the 1980s, near the end of Walker's term, social issues as never before began to come before the city's attention. Issues like homelessness, teenage delinquency, and spousal abuse were now topics of discussion—although solutions were left mainly for private institutions to solve.

During her early years on the council, before the State Open Meetings Act was passed, the council would meet for private discussions at restaurants like Cattleman's, Quality Inn Cibola, and for barbeque at Red Bryan's. After many council meetings, some council members would go out and relax at an ice cream parlor. [11]

During the 1970s there was always the looming issue of the Seven Seas Park. The city's political system and priorities had never come in for such scrutiny. The *Arlington Daily News*, most precisely reporter Christine Wicker, wrote long stories examining the economics of Seven Seas. The *Fort Worth Star-Telegram* as well had long, critical articles written by reporter Z. Joe Thornton. Likewise, the *Dallas Morning News* had long pieces on the Seven Seas issue.[12]

By the time of her departure from the council in 1982, the old guard politics of the city was having a rough time. "The 'movers and shakers' were no longer moving and shaking quite so much." [13]

Another city council election the same year as the Thompson-Walker race, 1972, can be interpreted as the most revealing. In this contest, local elites openly battled with one another, and the fallout from this political battle would be felt for some time later.

Paul Yarbrough, a longtime city resident, was an independently wealthy entrepreneur and developer. He was at odds with some of the decisions being made by the council, especially that of the Seven Seas project which was launched the same year.

The Yarbrough supporters were primarily against the city involving itself with a venture they believed better suited to private enterprise. Yarbrough was able to enlist some local establishment figures to aid in his campaign, notably James Cribbs. James Cribbs was another longtime resident and prominent attorney. His father, Ott Cribbs, had been police chief from 1934 to 1972.

James Cribbs had been an active member of the Republican party for much of his adult life; he later became a member of the State Republican Executive Committee. It is likely that if Cribbs had wanted the position, he could have become the party chairman.

James Cribbs was an early and consistent supporter of Tom Vandergriff. But the 1972 election tested that support severely. Paul Yarbrough was a client of the Cribbs law firm. James Cribbs and Paul Yarbrough had played football together and went to the same high school.

James Cribbs, like Yarbrough, never believed the city should be in the water theme park business.[14] Paul Yarbrough had other quarrels with the city as well. He disliked, as a developer, what he considered many needless standards and restrictions on commercial development.

Paul Yarbrough filed for Place 4 on the council, a seat that was previously held by Willard Sutton, who decided not to file for re-election. Paul Yarbrough never went to visit with Mayor Vandergriff about his candidacy as so many had done before.

Paul Yarbrough was a man known for his independence and entrepreneurship. He felt it demeaning to have to ask for Mayor Vandergriff's acknowledgment to run for city council. He would not, as he put it, "go after the mayor's blessing!"[15]

After this filing by Yarbrough, the political lines were drawn. The Vandergriff forces believed this was a direct attempt to challenge their decision-making, so they would back a candidate who they believed could defeat Yarbrough—Ralph Shelton.

Ralph Shelton says that he approached Mayor Vandergriff about running against Yarbrough. Others say that it was really Mayor Vandergriff who urged Ralph Shelton to run against Yarbrough.[16]

Ralph Shelton had been in Arlington since 1966 and had

James Cribbs (21 March 1979).
—*Fort Worth Star-Telegram* Photograph Collection
Special Collections Division
The University of Texas at Arlington Libraries

immersed himself in real estate before becoming politically motivated. He attended the University of Texas at Arlington. It was, he says, the sales tax elections in the city and the controversies surrounding the subject that brought him to politics.[17]

He was appointed early on to the Zoning Board of Adjustment. In the late 1960s, he helped to found the "Young Men for Arlington" and actively worked as a builder and developer for candidates endorsed by that group. And in 1970, he became president of the Arlington Board of Realtors.[18]

His principal supporters in the heated contest against Paul Yarbrough, aside from Mayor Tom Vandergriff, were: a large part of the real estate community, Tom Cravens (banking and real estate), James Luttrell (investor), and James "Big Daddy" Knapp, (investor and landowner). Many old time residents and families in Arlington were split in their support for these two candidates.[19]

The election was a contest of signed support ads in newspapers, mail-outs, yard signs, and endorsement cards. For weeks Arlington residents were curious about whose name appeared on which campaign endorsement literature. Citizens who normally would have little interest in city political matters were drawn to this council race. It was a clean election in that no personal diatribes were engaged. It was just a hard fought, down-to-the-wire contest from start to finish.

Ralph Shelton eventually came out victorious in an extremely close election. Paul Yarbrough never ran again for local political office and later dedicated much of his time to state and national political causes.

The rift between those who supported Shelton and those who supported Yarbrough eventually healed. But it was not an easy political wound to mend. And it was the most serious challenge from within the establishment ever to Mayor Tom Vandergriff's political base.

Even though James Cribbs supported Paul Yarbrough in this 1972 election, he never lost admiration for Tom Vandergriff. He credits Tom Vandergriff for much of the city's growth. "Arlington was able to grow due in part to the reduced level of controversy. There was little factionalism and no attempts at recall elections." [20]

Both James Cribbs and George Hawkes atttribute much of Arlington's growth to a consensus among city leaders and very little disagreement among elites on the course of the city. This contrasts sharply with increased factionalism and splintering among elites in Grand Prairie during the period when Arlington was growing rapidly.[21]

Sam Hamlett

Sam Hamlett was a longtime friend of Betty and Nile Fischer. For many years he and his family lived one block away from the Fischer family in a small home in central Arlington. Like the Fischers he had been very active in Democratic Party politics. He had worked very hard in the losing effort by Homer Rainey, a former president of the University of Texas at Austin, to become governor of Texas.

Sam Hamlett, a World War II combat veteran, was a member of a plane crew shot down in the Pacific. After the war he attended the University of Texas at Austin. There he obtained his Ph.D. in political science, but really termed himself an historian. His specialty was local government. He had amazing recall of political and historical events in Texas.

Early in his life he had lived in a part of South Texas, which at the time had a colorful and often suspect political system. He was always able to infuse his class lectures with his observations of South Texas politics, especially the infamous 1948 election of Lyndon Baines Johnson to the United States Senate.

He had visited Arlington as early as 1947, but he did not come to live in the community until 1956, when he came as a professor of government to Arlington State College. He was employed by E.C. Barksdale, who was at the time the head of a large combined social studies department at what was then known as Arlington State College. E.C. Barksdale and his wife, Marge, were also active in Democratic politics. Marge Barksdale was most influential early on in encouraging a young Jim Wright to run for the United States Congress.

Sam Hamlett always exhibited a quiet, gentle, and scholarly demeanor. Perhaps his greatest political strength and human trait was in attempting to understand the political actions of people. In this light he was usually forgiving, unless a politician had grossly overstepped legal and moral boundaries.

In 1959 he began to teach classes in urban government at Arlington State College. Viewing the growth and politics of the city of Arlington was, in many ways, a case study for him and his students.

Most of his participation at the time, however, was in partisan politics, attending and leading Democratic precinct conventions, and attending district and state conventions. He ventured into the Arlington political scene in the mid-1960s when

Sam Hamlett, circa 1970.
—Photo courtesy of Sam Hamlett

he, the Fischers, and others strongly opposed and were successful in blocking an attempt by city leaders to levy a one cent sales tax. A sales tax, however, was later successfully passed.

In 1977 Sam Hamlett considered running for the Arlington City Council. He had lived in the city for two decades, knew its political system well, and was acquainted with many of its leaders. He believed that city politics was becoming a bit more fluid with the resignation of Mayor Vandergriff and the vacancy in one of the council positions.

Sam Hamlett had the support of several community leaders who had broad establishment ties as well. James Cribbs, a prominent local attorney, and Paul Yarbrough, an independently wealthy landowner and entrepreneur, joined his support ranks. Betty Fischer, other Democratic party stalwarts, and some parts of the university community gave Sam Hamlett a solid base.

There were several candidates in the contest for the open place on the council. A run-off was needed between Hamlett and Don Wolfe, with Hamlett emerging victorious. Sam Hamlett's tenure on the council lasted two years. In that period of time the main issues were to build back the infrastructure that he felt had been neglected.

The financial picture in Arlington needed attention and the city's bond rating was in jeopardy. However, the bond rating did improve later and the continued growth allowed the city to avoid more serious financial problems.

While on the city council, Sam Hamlett advocated a broadening of representation on city boards and commissions and the opening up of public buildings for political meetings. In 1978 Ken Groves was elected to the council, and the public began to perceive that these two men were political allies.

The alliance of Ken Groves and Sam Hamlett was not by design, but their commonly held views about city growth, infrastructure, and the opening up of boards and commissions to a more diverse group brought them together.

Both Hamlett and Groves were tagged by more established interests as being against growth, and this was always a serious and sensitive issue with local elites. They never got together on how to vote and occasionally Hamlett would vote against Groves on policies he brought before the council.

But when Sam Hamlett decided to run for re-election in 1979 his perceived alliance with Ken Groves hurt him politically. The year 1979 witnessed one of the town's bitterest elections. Ken Groves had managed to place the issues of single-member districts and civil service system on the ballot.

The two volatile referendums on the ballot were detrimental to Hamlett's re-election campaign. Those against single-member districts and a civil service system for police and fire personnel would vote against Hamlett as well. He had always favored these two issues and they worked against him in his re-election attempt.

His main opponent was a retired military officer, Leo Berman, though there were others, including political activist Harry Robinson. Leo Berman had wide name recognition for having run in 1978 as a Republican for the United States

Congress. He lost the election for Congress, but then turned his attention to city politics.

Leo Berman was able to translate his support in his earlier congressional election into city council campaign support. The council election was very close, forcing a later run-off between Sam Hamlett and Leo Berman. Berman won the close run-off election, and would go on to serve three consecutive full terms until deciding not to run for re-election in 1985.

During the 1979 run-off election, Sam Hamlett alleged that the Berman campaign had hired people through the "Kelly Girls" employment agency to be at voting places in an effort to hear names of those who had voted. If some of their potential supporters had not voted, they would be called and told to vote.

Hamlett contended this was in violation of the state election code and complained to the city secretary's office, which ordered the "Kelly Girls" to leave the voting places. Subsequently, Sam Hamlett filed a complaint with the District Attorney's Office but was informed "It was not something to pursue very effectively." Leo Berman replied that he knew nothing of the "Kelly Girl" episode, and the matter faded.[22]

Ken Groves

Perhaps of all the council members during the time period of this study, Ken Groves was the most vilified and yet respected. After being elected to the council in 1978 with his defeat of Richard Greene, some members of the establishment never forgave him.

Ken Groves was by profession an engineer and a surveyor. Earlier he had held the office of county surveyor, which was later abolished. This occupation placed him in a position to know politicians and the political landscape in the area. Further, he had come from a political family.

He was usually soft spoken, serious, and deliberate. As a council member he would study reports and agenda items thoroughly. When a cable television franchise came before the council for the first time, he spent many weeks studying reports and consulting with advisors over which company to choose.

He had a diverse coterie of close friends from every walk of life. One of his best friends was Harry Robinson, a libertarian intellectual who was often at odds with the council. Early in his business career, Ken Groves had befriended Mount Olive Baptist Church, a predominately African-American congregation.

He would often attend church services at Mount Olive. He extended friendship and engineering and surveying expertise to this congregation. This was done in the 1950s when the black population was very small and not as politically significant as it would become in later years. His name is on the cornerstone of the new Mount Olive Baptist Church in the center of the city. His funeral service was held at Mount Olive Baptist Church with their famous pastor, Reverend N.L. Robinson, delivering an emotional good-bye to their friend.[23]

Though a devout Baptist, he was a man curious about other religions and ways of life. He reveled in discussions of political ideas and was acquainted with the great political philosophers John Locke, John Stuart Mill, and Jeremy Bentham. He could cite passages from the Federalist Papers.

After a few years on the council, he began to win the respect of council members who had viewed him suspiciously. And in turn he showed his fondness for Arlington and his pride in being on the council. He often would wear a blue tie with the Arlington logo imprinted on it.

After a time, local elites—bankers, real estate, and developers—began to seek him out for advice. And all through his council years at almost every function, including the formal council sessions, he would be accompanied by his wife of many years, Jeanette.

From the late 1970s through the late 1980s, Ken Groves debated the issues of mass transit (which he opposed), cable television franchises, streets, an improved water system, and revitalization of east Arlington. And he often speculated as early as the 1970s about transforming Johnson Creek into a river walk of some type to enhance its image.

During his multiple council terms he prided himself in being able to solve problems in unique ways. For years teenagers had been driving up and down Cooper Street near the university

Ken Groves at a city council meeting (22 November 1979).
—*Fort Worth Star-Telegram* Photograph Collection
Special Collections Division
The University of Texas at Arlington Libraries

area on weekends. The teen motorcade had become so bad that traffic was affected and detours for regular travel often had to be arranged. Cooper Street became known throughout the metropolitan area, especially in the late 1970s through the early 1980s, as the place to be for teens and their cars.

Predictably, neighbors complained of noise, littering, loitering, and occasionally fights. The police would routinely try to control the maddening scene, but no real solution occurred. Ken Groves implemented a plan to try and alleviate the traffic congestion by arranging for bands, restrooms, and soft drinks on a nearby University of Texas at Arlington parking lot with hopes of luring the teens out of their cars.

Ken Groves' idea was a success with the teens. The city would routinely clean up the mess left by the teens. Soon the traffic jams eased, and Cooper Street was no longer the place for teens to drive up and down looking for fun and occasionally trouble. Cooper Street returned to its normal state of affairs. He also worked to lower Cooper Street and build above-street pedestrian walkways at the point it traveled through the University of Texas at Arlington campus.

Ken Groves had a keen eye for new people to serve on boards, commissions, and the council itself. In the late 1980s, he became friends with Elzie Odom. Groves held a series of receptions for Elzie Odom, testing his possible support for a council run. Buoyed by this support, Ken Groves urged Elzie Odom to run for the council. Eventually, Odom was successful and became a council member and later mayor. Elzie Odom became the first African American on the council and the first African American mayor of the city.

At the end of his political career Ken Groves declared his race for the office of county judge of the Tarrant County Commissioners Court. He was to run in the Democratic primary when he died unexpectedly. Due to the timing of death his name was still on the ballot, and he received enough votes to win the primary. The fact that a deceased man won an election became a media sensation.

If Ken Groves had lived to run in the general election, his Republican opponent would have been Tom Vandergriff.

Jim Norwood

All through the era of this study there was no more controversial or colorful personality on the city council than Jim Norwood. During this time he was owner of an automobile paint company. His notoriety or fame, depending on the viewer's perspective, was known all through the metropolitan area.

He was first elected to the council in 1984 on strictly economic issues. A homeowner's association was upset at street assessments and he championed their cause. But soon after his election to the council, his attention turned to social issues. And it was on these issues that he became well known.

Theatre Arlington was a local theatre company that was already becoming recognized for the quality of its productions. A group not directly affiliated with Theatre Arlington but using its facilities planned to open a version of Edward Albee's

"Who's Afraid of Virginia Woolfe" with homosexual overtones. Jim Norwood, a council member for a short time, immediately criticized the play for its performances in Arlington.

Theatre Arlington at the time had not received any public funds, nor was this proposed production of "Virginia Woolfe" one of their own season plays.[24] Nevertheless, Jim Norwood felt compelled to criticize the theatre for daring to allow it to be produced on their stage.

After his criticism became known throughout the community, the controversy continued and broadened. Richard Greene, then a first-term council member, was at the time a member of the Board of Directors of Theater Arlington. He resigned from the board over their upcoming production.

The episode and criticism of a local theatre group became so notorious that it made international news.[25] Edward Albee himself became involved and demanded that the play not be produced in the homosexual context saying it would distort his original intent. The production stirred up so much controversy and debate that it was never presented on the Theatre Arlington stage.

Jim Norwood's social agenda broadened to other issues. A large park in Arlington, Randol Mill Park, had become known in the media as a place where homosexuals would occasionally gather. Jim Norwood would ride with Arlington police to the park to see if homosexuals were violating any city ordinances or state laws. His riding with the police also became widely publicized.

As a council member he began meeting with a city staff member, city planner Bruce McClendon, to write a city ordinance that would tightly restrict "adult entertainment video stores" in the city.

When the ordinance was formally proposed it created great controversy and debate with many citizens making comments before the city council and in area newspapers. The majority of the citizen remarks were in favor of the ordinance. At one city council meeting, the room was packed with supporters of the restrictive ordinance. Dozens spoke in favor, with only one citizen at the end of the evening talking about First Amendment protections.

Jim Norwood (7 August 1984).
—*Fort Worth Star-Telegram* Photograph Collection
Special Collections Division
The University of Texas at Arlington Libraries

One adult video store manager at a council public hearing revealed that in Arlington there was a great demand for adult video rentals. Many of the participants at city council meetings told the council that "They spoke for the citizens of Arlington that did not want X-rated videos sold in Arlington stores." The seated audience would often break into wild applause. This left one to wonder just who in Arlington was doing all the renting of these videos? And who really could speak for the citizens of the city?

Later, it was determined by the city legal department that the proposed ordinance would never pass constitutional scrutiny. It was written in too broad a language and if challenged would most likely be struck down by the courts. The adult video ordinance was dropped.

However, in the coming weeks a few video store operators complained that they were now being harassed by city police who would allegedly drop by to check on other city ordinance enforcement. The city denied that there was any harassment.

Jim Norwood then turned his attention to what he considered to be pornographic magazines in some convenience stores. He protested by picketing outside some stores and urging them not to sell some of the magazines they had for sale. The convenience chain stores relented and placed some of the designated magazines behind the counter away from full view.

For his entire term of office, Jim Norwood continued to raise the public ire. He became a constant subject for either ridicule or praise in his quest to rid Arlington of material or activities he considered to be objectionable, immoral, illicit, or pornographic.

He even criticized some male city employees for wearing earrings. This remark, like so many others, became well known by the public through the media. He became so well known for his criticisms that the *Dallas Morning News* devoted an entire magazine section to him.

The basis for Jim Norwood's comments originated, he said, from his fundamentalist Christian underpinnings. He sincerely believed that homosexuality, pornography, and other immoral activities (by his definition) were injurious to the community.

Jim Norwood was a very amicable person. He never shouted nor ever verbally scolded any citizen. Indeed, he was often joyful and had a good sense of humor. Yet his term on the council was full of controversy and debate. The city of Arlington was becoming well known nationwide by his comments and actions while on the council.

Some in the city felt that he was hurting Arlington's image and might even curtail tourism to town. In 1986 he lost his re-election bid to Dick Malec. And in 1987, trying to regain a council position, he lost again to Larry Walther. He left the political arena for the pulpit.

He became a voluntary chaplain with the Tarrant County Jail, to serve as spiritual leader of what was popularly known as the "God Pod." Norwood was a founder of "Families in Crisis" in Fort Worth and also became a pastor in a Kennedale Church Oak Crest Baptist Church.

Whatever citizens of the time thought of his criticisms and remarks, he was never accused of being hypocritical.

Richard (Dick) Malec

In 1986 Dick Malec, with the support of many citizens who believed Jim Norwood had gone too far in his repeated societal criticisms, defeated his opponent in the scheduled election. The election pivoted primarily on Jim Norwood and his record. Dick Malec garnered some business support from those who belived Jim Norwood had the potential of harming the city's reputation as a tourist town.

Dick Malec's three-term tenure on the council was itself at times controversial as well as confrontational. He had strong ideas about how city government should be run. And very often they came into conflict with established patterns. His criticism of city government operations pivoted over how council members were to conduct city business. Specifically, he wanted to be able to talk to administrative staff instead of having to route all communication through the city manager's office.[26]

Some believed he wanted to usurp the city manager's responsibilities under the council-manager form of government, which was a hallmark of the city. Dick Malec countered saying "I was not worried about running the city instead of the city manager, I just wanted to talk to other city staff."[27]

The conflict was never completely resolved. There was much tension at city council work sessions between the city manager Bill Kirchoff and Dick Malec. Much of the city council was drawn into the continuing struggle between these two strong personalities.

Later, Dick Malec rallied much citizen support by taking the position that the city staff could be performing many of the tasks that consultants were being hired to perform. Too many consultants, not enough staff work.

Malec won favor with various constituencies in the city by taking the position that the city was trying to over-regulate. He was at odds with fellow councilman Roger "Rocky" Walton, whom Malec labeled "Rocky Regulator." "Rocky" Walton at the time was in favor of many new regulatory ordinances.

Dick Malec (15 March 1985).
—*Fort Worth Star-Telegram* Photograph Collection
Special Collections Division
The University of Texas at Arlington Libraries

In 1992 Dick Malec, in a re-election bid for a fourth term, was defeated by Dixon Holman. Dixon Holman was the son of a well-known and longtime Arlington family. His father, who had the same name, was a respected former council member who later became a state judge.

Those opposed to Malec said he had become divisive and confrontational. The campaign was a hard fought one. It was never easy to unseat an incumbent. However, Dixon Holman won the election and Dick Malec returned to private business.

For a time, many constituencies in Arlington lamented the absence of Dick Malec from the council. Bumper stickers briefly appeared inscribed with "I Miss Malec!"

George Hawkes

George Hawkes always played a prominent role in Arlington city politics. Perhaps only second to Tom Vandergriff, he was "the man to see" about political support from the early 1950s through the 1970s. His prominence derived from his position as the editor and publisher of the city's premier local paper, the *Citizen-Journal*.

But George Hawkes was more than simply an editor and publisher. Since his early arrival in Arlington he had developed a large following. He was an astute businessman and a loyal and longtime member of the First Baptist Church. If someone were casting a movie about a small- to medium-sized town in postwar America, surely he could have played the role of a benevolent, no-nonsense civic booster and pillar of the community.

He was a southern gentleman, usually seen in a suit, tie, and a hat slightly tilted to one side. George Hawkes came to Arlington in 1946 as a veteran of World War II. He was a man of conservative bearing, always proper in dress and appearance.

When he arrived, the population of Arlington was about 6,500. W.F. Altman was the mayor. Mayor Altman had been a city councilman in 1934 and 1935, and then served twelve years in the mayor's office until 1947. He would be succeeded by B.C. Barnes.

In 1947 Mayor Barnes was the business manager at North Texas Agricultural College, later known as Arlington State, and ultimately the University of Texas at Arlington. Mayor Barnes would be defeated by Tom Vandergriff in 1951.

The two newspapers were the *Arlington Citizen* and the *Arlington Journal* and they were very competitive. Soon after arrival Hawkes purchased the *Arlington Citizen*. In 1957 the two papers merged into one corporation as the *Citizen-Journal* and became the premier local paper for decades.

When George Hawkes arrived in Arlington there was a volunteer fire department, and there were some large fires that often strained the fledgling department to its capacity. In the downtown area a large pole with a red light atop would summon extra fire and police help if needed.

George Hawkes, Publisher, Arlington Citizen Journal (30 June 1968).
Fort Worth Star-Telegram Photograph Collection
Special Collections Division
The University of Texas at Arlington Libraries

In the 1940s, prior to and immediately after his arrival, there was still the old style of political speechmaking in the community. "Politicians would gather around election time and stand on a flat-bed truck and speak."[28] The Downtown Rotary Club, which dates to 1923, was very important politically when George Hawkes arrived in town in 1946. It would remain so for another four decades.

Benton Collins was the city secretary then. He was a powerful city secretary, assuming many administrative responsibilities for over fourteen years, from 1934 to 1947. According to George Hawkes he played a large role in "running the city." He was almost assuming the role of a city manager, though not formally having the title.[29] Arlington did not have a city manager position until 1950.

George Hawkes was never on the city council, although he was asked to run for the council at least several times from the late 1950s to the 1970s. He always declined. He did serve on the Dallas Fort Worth Turnpike Commission, because to him the Turnpike was pivotal to Arlington's growth.[30]

Arlington always had strong representation on the Turnpike Commission. Other Arlington citizens who served on the Dallas Fort Worth Turnpike Commission at various times were Clyde Ashworth and Al Rollins.[31]

George Hawkes, like other early observers, credits Arlington's growth to its political stability and leadership consensus. "Grand Prairie in the 1940s had much more than Arlington. It had North American Aviation and military facilities which Arlington did not."[32]

Arlington leaders, both elected and non-elected, did not need to have many formal and highly structured meetings to arrive at decisions. The major goals were generally understood. There may have been disagreements on specifics, but not on the overall goals. According to Hawkes, "We all had basic agreements, knew pretty well what each other was thinking."[33] However, Grand Prairie at the time had too many factions and divisions that impeded its continued growth. "The two main banks there were always fighting."[34]

In Arlington the two main banks, Arlington State Bank (later to become Arlington Bank and Trust) and First National were very competitive, but not hostile to one another. There was competition over which bank would receive school district and city funds, so they alternated with one another on which would receive the funds.[35] From the 1950s, and for several decades thereafter, school and city bond elections passed rather easily. Rarely was there any opposition.[36]

George Hawkes remembers some early political conflicts over liquor sales. After prohibition ended and the state allowed local option, the city allowed beer sales, but only after a bitter battle. In the early 1900s, according to the city secretary's office, there were five saloons on East Main alone. Later, Arlington became a "dry" city in the 1920s along with national prohibition.

Eventually, liquor was allowed to be sold "by the glass" in

licensed restaurants and bars. However, while the city has never sanctioned package liquor stores, there are liquor stores at the fringes of the city limits. These conflicts never tore at the consensus that was emerging in the city.

In the late 1940s, George Hawkes, becoming an established leader in the community, received a letter from a young Arlingtonite attending the University of Southern California.

The college student wrote to Hawkes about newspaper coverage of high school football games. A few years later, Hawkes would help recruit and encourage the young man, upon arriving back in town, to run for mayor. He had already served a brief term as head of the chamber of commerce.

As mayor, Tom Vandergriff would quickly set the tone for Arlington for years to come.[37] George Hawkes would always be there to support him.

For nearly four decades George Hawkes was an important voice in the community. Through his church, newspaper, and reputation he was indispensable to the establishment. The Central Library in downtown Arlington bears his name.

Dr. R.G. "Wick" Alexander

Dr. R.G. "Wick" Alexander thought about running for the United States Congress at one time. He also had speculated on running for mayor of Arlington. Neither idea was far fetched at the time. He was, during the late 1960s through the decade of the 1970s, one of Arlington's most active community leaders and promising politicians.

Dr. R. G. "Wick" Alexander was a prominent orthodontist in the community. He established his practice in July 1964. His early record of civic involvement provided a textbook perfect platform for political office. He was active in the YMCA, Big Brothers, and later the United Way Campaign, Arlington Human Service Planners, and Leadership Arlington.

He was asked by community leaders to run for election to the Arlington School Board, but decided instead to focus on city politics. He was appointed first to the Planning and Zoning Commission, then he approached Mayor Tom Vandergriff about running for city council and was encouraged to make the race.

"Wick" Alexander
—Photo courtesy of Wick Alexander

His first campaign for city council was in 1971 for Place 3, which did not have an incumbent running at the time. Six other candidates were vying for the open spot. His main opponent was Betty Fischer. There was no provision for a run-off at the time and Dr. Alexander won the close election.

His election to the council followed the traditional path. He garnered the support of James Martin, superintendent of Arlington Public Schools. Even though he was not running for a school board position, the informal support of the school district was always a great help to candidates.

A steering committee was established with many of the same prominent names that were shown on other steering committees in the past. He drew the support of many members from the prominent churches at the time. First Methodist and First Baptist were always politically prominent. The real estate community, led by Billie Farrar, was there to help. And then there were the traditional newspaper ads with assorted names listed. And even yard signs with "Pick Wick" as a slogan to motivate voters.

Dr. Alexander had been a Republican early in his life. Even though the council is elected on a non-partisan basis, he did become the first Republican ever elected to the council. Several decades later, with the Republican Party more dominant, there would be other Republicans represented on the council.

Dr. Alexander served on the council from 1971 to 1977. During this period the public water system was enhanced and trash collection streamlined, and the waste disposal and landfill expanded. There were issues that he believed were overlooked as well—the library system, animal control, and a more modern sanitary animal control facility. These issues would only be addressed later in the 1980s to 1990s.

The animal control facility, which existed for much of the city's history, was located near a creek that often flooded the buildings. They were euthanized in the cruelest of ways. Dogs and cats were routinely herded into an old building and gases were piped in from automobile exhausts to euthanize them. It was a municipal responsibility, but certainly not one of high priority.

Dr. Alexander was attentive to these problems and helped out of his own resources to update the area. Later, in the 1980s, the city would build a new animal facility and update its euthanasia procedures.

One of the most heated issues during his council tenure was the proposal by the city's Planning Board to widen Fielder Road from south of Park Row to immediately north of Division. Dr. Alexander favored the widening proposal and was booed at neighborhood meetings for his support of the project.

Most council members were at first in favor of the expansion. They believed, as did the planners, that another north-south thoroughfare was needed. However, the political pressure from the affected homeowners was so great that they reversed their position and the widening of that part of Fielder never occurred.[38] This was a homeowner victory, but the need for more north-south traffic arteries went largely unanswered.

Even though they did not serve on the city council at the same time, Dr. Alexander believes that Ken Groves was instrumental in changing the nature of city politics. "Ken Groves changed the council forever. He went public with issues which earlier council members did not do."[39] This meant that Ken Groves would talk to the media, civic and neighborhood associations about issues, conflicts, and personalities that formerly were kept among council members themselves.[40]

Near the end of Dr. Alexander's service on the council, 1977, there was an assumption on the part of some leaders that S.J. Stovall would serve a full elected term and then not run again. This would allow Dr. Alexander to attempt a run for the mayor's position. However, these assumptions never materialized.[41]

Dr. Alexander would leave the city council, but he would remain active in a wide variety of civic duties.

James Martin

James Martin was superintendent of Arlington Public Schools from 1955 to 1976. This period coincided with the Vandergriff era. James Martin was close friends with Tom Vandergriff and George Hawkes. In fact, James Martin was very friendly with almost every establishment leader for four decades. He and his wife, Eleanor Grace Martin, were neighbors to Billie Farrar, who was a very important leader in the real estate community and worker in selected council campaigns.

After retiring from his superintendent's position, James Martin became Honorary Chairman of Tom Vandergriff's two congressional campaigns in 1982 and 1984.

James Martin was able to combine an almost cherubic personality with strict administrative responsibilities. He always stressed that his duties and role as superintendent divorced him from city politics. He emphasized that city politics had little to do with school politics.[42]

Technically he was correct. But informally there was always an important and vital connection between the politics of the school district and that of the city. School and city personalities often intersected in church and civic clubs.

James Martin, Superintendent of Arlington Independent School District (18 July 1979).

—*Fort Worth Star-Telegram* Photograph Collection
Special Collections Division
The University of Texas at Arlington Libraries

James Martin, superintendent of schools, George Hawkes, editor and publisher, S.J. Stovall, mayor, and Harold Patterson, mayor, all were prominent members of First Baptist Church. Many of these same powerful city leaders were likewise members of the same civic clubs, notably the Downtown Rotary that met at the First United Methodist Church. The Vandergriff family was a longtime member of the First United Methodist Church.

James Martin was a close friend with several Arlington city managers, council members, and mayors. Before becoming superintendent, Martin was principal of Arlington High School. While Martin was principal at the high school, Harold Patterson, later to become mayor, was a student there. Similarly, Ken Groves, Barton Thompson, Tom Cravens, and Dr. Eugene Pope were students there during James Martin's term as a high school principal. All of these men would become important community and political leaders.

School employees, including administration, staff, and teachers were occasionally motivated to participate in city affairs. Growth was emphasized for the school district as well as for the city. If the school district did not grow, there would be less need for teachers and administrators. If fewer people came to town, that would endanger the property tax base and in turn affect the school district adversely.

City real estate interests used the growth and development of the school district as an asset for residential and commercial sales. Occasionally a real estate sales sign would proudly proclaim, "Within Arlington School District." City politics, school politics, and interests very often converged. For a time both school and city property taxes were collected by the city.

During the tenure of James Martin as superintendent no school bond issue ever failed with the exception of one part of a larger bond package. That was a swimming pool proposition, which was defeated. While mayor, Tom Vandergriff supported all school bond proposals. And in turn school officials individually supported all city bond issues.[43]

When superintendent Martin retired in 1976, he was given a large retirement celebration that was attended by many city political leaders, community leaders, as well as school personnel. A large high school in the city now bears his name.

Dottie Lynn

One of the longest serving members of the city council was Dottie Lynn. She was elected in 1982, vacated her seat to run for mayor in 1987, returned to the council a year later, and served until 2000.

Dottie Lynn was among the many council members recruited by Mayor Tom Vandergriff to enter the political arena. In 1976 the mayor asked her to serve on the Planning and Zoning Commission, usually a gateway to the council.

She served on the commission for six years before running for council in 1982. Martha Walker, the first woman to be elected to the council, had decided not to run again for her

Place 5 position. Dottie Lynn decided to run for the open position with the support and encouragement of her family.

Dottie Lynn had come to Arlington in 1952 with her husband, who worked for Bell Helicopter. She was soft-spoken with a serious demeanor. Like Betty Fischer (who lost a close council race), Martha Walker, and Carolyn Snider, who were elected before her, Dottie Lynn helped pave the route for female representation on the city council. There had always been numerous women working "behind the scenes" politically, but these women brought female representation, power, and prestige up front and public.

The 1982 campaign for city council found Dottie Lynn against her principal opponent, Graham Schadt. Graham Schadt was a developer and was also well known and respected in the community. Martha Walker, however, campaigned for Graham Schadt primarily because of one principal issue also on the ballot at the time.

The city wanted to construct a convention center on part of the location of the old Seven Seas theme park. It was a controversial and sensitive issue. Some believed it too would fail given the failure of the theme park. Others believed it was doomed to failure if constructed since it could not, they thought, compete with Dallas and Fort Worth for convention goers.

Martha Walker as a member of the city council favored the convention center construction. Dottie Lynn opposed it, fearing that the hotel-motel tax, known as the "bed tax," would not alone support it. Other revenues she believed at the time would be necessary for financing. This was the principal reason for Martha Walker's support of Graham Schadt over Dottie Lynn.

The convention center issue passed, but in a very close vote total. And Dottie Lynn would prevail over Graham Schadt in a close vote total as well. The convention center proved to be a successful venture and in 1999 a large addition to it was constructed.

After vacating her council seat in 1987 she would run for mayor. In a hard fought campaign she lost to Richard Greene. After her losing mayoral try she would remain off the council for one year, then run and win her council place back. She

Dottie Lynn (8 November 1984).
—*Fort Worth Star-Telegram* Photograph Collection
Special Collections Division
The University of Texas at Arlington Libraries

then remained on the council until the year 2000, at which time she voluntarily relinquished her place in the next election cycle.

Her tenure as a member of the Planning and Zoning Board for six years in the mid to late 1970s was characterized by problems with zoning. Some land was changing hands so rapidly by a process known as "land flipping" that zoning was difficult and divisive. As a council member her most notable achievement was the vision and tenacity she had in the construction of Green Oaks Boulevard, which now encircles the city.

As a council member she characterized herself as a "homeowner's" advocate. As a council member she served with three different mayors, Stovall, Patterson, and Greene. She remembers that "There was an ongoing tension between Harold Patterson and Ken Groves as there was between Dick Malec and the then city manager, Bill Kirchoff." [44]

Dottie Lynn, however, credits Bill Kirchoff with important administrative changes. "Bill Kirchoff had new ideas. He brought in cost-benefit analysis for development. Kirchoff predicted the recession starting in the mid-1980s and cost cutting was advocated. He also brought in many females to head up city departments." [45]

Dottie Lynn always had enough loyal community supporters to elect her to a council place, but not enough to elect her as mayor. After her retirement from her long service on the council, a large reception was held to honor her at the city convention center. At that event, Tom Vandergriff, who recruited her for the Planning and Zoning Board, and the three mayors she served with as a council member all applauded her work.

A city recreation center in the Woodland West housing addition now bears her name, as does a portion of Green Oaks Boulevard, the thoroughfare she championed.

Kelly Jones

In 1985 Kelly Jones was a well-known and prominent attorney in town when he was elected to city council after a runoff election. He enlisted the support of many of the same community leaders, like Howard Wilemon, that so many others had previously courted for support.

His first campaign featured him running against Jen Barney, another longtime citizen of the city and community leader, and Jake Kennard, a local businessman. It was for a place on the council previously held by Leo Berman, who had chosen not to run again. Jones chose to hold his seat in 1987, but faced opposition from Bill McFadin, a former assistant fire chief in the city whom Jones defeated. In 1989 Kelly Jones decided not to run again and to devote more time to his growing legal practice. Bill McFadin ran for this place, and this time he won the election.

Kelly Jones (15 March 1985).
Fort Worth Star-Telegram *Photograph Collection*
Special Collections Division
The University of Texas at Arlington Libraries

Kelly Jones was raised in Arlington and knew its political landscape well. His close-up observations of city politics as a council member took on a studied and professorial perspective.

In the 1950s to 1970s, when Kelly Jones was growing up in the city, ministers and their churches were of more political importance than later. The First Baptist and First United Methodist Church were important due to their large and influential memberships. As the population grew and more diversified religious congregations entered the community, political power emanating from churches became more dispersed.

In 1985, for his first council campaign, Jones enlisted the support of Bryan Eppstein, a professional campaign consultant, to help in the run-off phase of his successful race. The use of professionals to help manage and run campaigns became more frequent during this time period. Campaigning for city council was now resembling that of more professionally run state and national elections.

Kelly Jones was a member of the council at the same time the economy of the state and the city was in a downturn. Oil prices had declined dramatically from the previous highs and land values, which had become inflated, were in decline. Bankruptcies were up and many developers were down. It was, he says, "a troubled time." [46]

He, like Dottie Lynn, credits Bill Kirchoff, the new city manager, for recognizing the downturn and preparing the city for it. In the mid-1980s, the city was beginning to change dramatically with the addition of new population groups.

He observes that Richard Greene as a member of the Planning and Zoning Board was very ideological in outlook, often unyielding. But beginning in 1987, as mayor he became more open, a true consensus builder who worked toward conciliation.[47]

Kelly Jones was only on the council for two terms. Second terms for council members are important as they give experience and expertise to the council. However, serving more than two terms may begin to wear down some politicians. The freshness and enthusiasm they had at first may diminish.[48]

Kelly Jones divides those who have held political office into two categories: those who like issues and those who simply like to govern. Perhaps, most politicians combine the two.

After leaving the city council he briefly considered running for a state senate seat previously held by Arlington attorney Bob McFarland. However, he decided not to run for this state office. In 1987 he was appointed to the Board of Regents for Stephen F. Austin College in Nacogdoches, Texas. Later, he became chairman of the Board of Regents for this prominent institution of higher learning.

Roger "Rocky" Walton

Roger "Rocky" Walton was another two-term council member who was first elected in 1990 when he ran for an open place on the council. He remained on the council until 1994 when his term expired. He then endorsed Judy Rupay for his council position and she was elected.

Known by his nickname "Rocky," he followed the time-worn path of many to the council. He was appointed to the Planning and Zoning Board and served there for nearly four years before running for the council.

Rocky Walton was a prominent personal injury attorney in Arlington. From 1975 until his election to the council in 1990, he practiced law with Roy English, who had been a state legislator and the presiding judge of the Tarrant County Commissioners Court.

Rocky Walton had been an active member of the Wimbledon Homeowner's Association. This group was interested in beautification for their neighborhood and the entire city. Throughout his political career the issue of beautification of the city and perceived "quality of life" issues would mark his tenure. Even before being elected to the council, while on the Planning and Zoning Board, he would favor a sidewalk ordinance in new developments.

During his years on the council, he became an advocate for the city library system, which he felt had been neglected in past years. He championed extended library hours, technological upgrades, and a bond issue to build and renovate libraries. All of these were successful ventures. While on the council he chaired the city council committee having oversight of library matters.

However, any controversy that developed during his terms of office did not stem from his advocacy of the library system. For other beautification and quality of life city ordinances, Rocky Walton would be given a tag name. Another council member, Dick Malec, would label him as "Rocky Regulator." The political debate over many of these issues lasted throughout his two terms on the council.

He strongly supported ordinances dealing with landscape, trees, and signs. He supported an ordinance to prohibit the posting of "For Sale" signs on public land. Most of his efforts were successful and took a practical dimension. He felt that a beautiful city would attract new business.

If his efforts at beautification were controversial, his initiation and sponsorship of anti-smoking ordinances would be even more heated. The anti-smoking ordinance was at the time one of the broadest in the country: no smoking in indoor public buildings; no smoking at sporting events, except in designated places; no smoking in restaurants, retail establishments, or movie theaters; and bars were exempt from the ordinance as well as restaurants which operated a proper ventilating system.

The ordinance drew much criticism from restaurant owners. Some Arlington protesters held a "smoke-in" to protest the ordinance. The new regulations were put in place and became a model for other cities.

Walton believes that Arlington politics has changed dramatically. "In early years, it was Board Room politics. The business establishment decided on candidates. But that has ended."[49]

As if the beautification and smoking ordinances did not generate enough controversy, there was still another issue. The Chamber of Commerce had been receiving money from the city for economic development issues. In 1992 Joe Ewen, then a city council member, was also chairman of the chamber board of directors. Rocky Walton felt this was too close a relationship between the chamber and the council and ultimately could lead to chamber control. He charged that Ted Willis, then the chamber's executive director, and the chamber were attempting to have a direct role in city politics.

Walton further believed that the chamber was trying to control the council by backing two candidates for council office in the early 1990s. Walton then demanded that because of perceived conflicts of interest and the chamber receiving city money the state Open Records Act should be applied. He called for and received a state attorney general's opinion that stated the Chamber of Commerce was a government entity and must comply with the Open Records Act.

Both the Open Records Act (passed in 1973) and the Open Meetings Act (first passed in 1967 and strengthened in 1973) greatly altered city politics. Walton recounts how the Open Meetings Act changed the political landscape. "When Harold Patterson was mayor one council member called him and said he had at least four votes to erect a Cross (Crucifix) to a city water tower. The mayor quickly informed the caller that any such discussion outside of a regularly scheduled council meeting was in violation of the Open Meetings Act." The conversation ended quickly.[50]

Kay Taebel

Kay Taebel came to Arlington in 1970 and immediately took an interest in city and school issues. Taebel believed that in order to run for office a person should live in the community awhile. So in three years she made her first try at elective office by running for a position on the Arlington School Board. She lost the first election to Dan Dipert, a prominent entrepreneur in the travel business. Then she ran against Dr. Truett Boles, a longtime pediatrician and school board member, and lost again. The loss of two school board races did not dim her political energy.

For the next two decades she would immerse herself in the politics of the community. She would be involved in a variety of issues, both school and city. Her main theme throughout the years was for more openness in government. She campaigned for more citizen involvement, checks on political power, and for term limits on city and school board positions, holding that power can be addictive.

For many years she would hold gatherings at her home to encourage candidates to run for office who were not, as she labeled them, the "chosen few."[51] And for a long while she would be successful in having lively citizen discussions at her home on various issues of community importance.

She had for many years been interested in implementation of some sort of single-member district plan for council members. Her husband, Del Taebel, was a professor at the University of

Kay Taebel, circa 1998.
Courtesy of Kay Taebel

Texas at Arlington's School of Urban and Public Affairs. He was a noted authority on different representation plans.

The long quest for some sort of city single-member district plan advocated by Kay Taebel and others would be successful. On November 2, 1993, a charter amendment election passed a plan that combined elements of the single-member district and at-large system. The referendum which was supported by a broad citizen alignment was spearheaded by a group called, "People for Accountable Government," headed by Kent Kirmser.[52]

She chose to campaign for a city council position and her main opponent was Rick Bondurant. The Bondurant family had been in the community for many years and had a variety of business interests. In a hard fought election she was able to defeat Rick Bondurant and take her seat on the council.

While on the council she continued to press for her long-held positions of more citizen participation and open government. She was able to implement cable television broadcasts of council work sessions traditionally held before the regular council meeting.

Due to a realignment of council positions made necessary by the new representation plan, Taebel would be in a close campaign with another council incumbent, Dan Serna. In a run-off election she would lose to him by 297 votes.

Kay Taebel brands the campaign against her as highly partisan. She was labeled a "liberal" in campaign literature. Her long support of single-member districts, smoking ordinances, and zoning restrictions hurt her election chances.[53]

She holds that then Mayor Richard Greene had a role in her defeat. "He promised he would stay out of the race, but he did not."[54] She considers Mayor Greene a very strong mayor. "Structurally and by city charter Arlington has a 'weak-mayor' system. But Greene was a very strong 'weak-mayor.'"[55]

Though critical of Mayor Greene for supporting her opponent she still credits him as being a good leader. The mayor physically sits in the middle and at the head of the council during meetings. The mayor introduces the subject and to some extent controls the time and length of debate. And Mayor Greene did all of these things well.[56]

However brief was Kay Taebel's stay on the council, her impact over several decades was strong. "She probably annoyed and bothered more council members and mayors over the years than anybody else in town. And that was a good thing, too."[57]

Tom Cravens

Tom Cravens was born to one of Arlington's most prominent and old families. Carlisle Cravens was his father who lived next door to the patriarch of the Vandergriff family, "Hooker" Vandergriff. Carlisle Cravens was on the Arlington school board as well as the State Board of Education.

Tom Cravens' great-grandfather's name, "Carlisle," adorned a much earlier version of what is now the University of Texas at Arlington. It was called "Carlisle Military Academy."

Tom Cravens himself has undertaken a number of civic and political roles, but never run for elective office. He had been asked at different times to run for city council, but also turned down the request. At one time he was president of the Arlington Chamber of Commerce and head of a city downtown renewal project. Since 1964, when he returned to Arlington from his college education at the University of Texas at Austin, Tom Cravens has been a person many have turned to for political help.

The elite establishment in Arlington has drawn its core membership from churches, civic clubs, corporate interests, real estate, developers, banking, and utility companies. Most certainly among the membership Tom Cravens' name must be included.

He has always been mild-mannered with a conservative political perspective. He has also been well regarded by those he has done business with in his role as an insurance and banking executive. He seems to relish his life in banking and insurance more than he desires any elected public office. For a time he was in the insurance business with a former council member, Wayne Coble.

His perspective on Arlington has been similar to other establishment leaders. He was very pro-growth. He wanted to attract corporations to the city. This philosophy fit in nicely with his role as a banker and civic leader.

He has favored consensus and non-divisive politics and the recruitment of council members who would fit this profile. He has argued that it was a cohesive city council coupled with strong mayoral leadership that developed the town.

The Cravens and Vandergriff families were political allies. At times their private enterprise and financial largesse was turned toward helping the city grow. This was certainly true of Hooker Vandergriff's financial role in helping to attract what is now the Texas Rangers baseball team.

In the late 1960s, just a bit earlier than when Arlington was beginning negotiations with the Washington Senators for relocation, negotiations were underway as well with the Texas College of Osteopathic Medicine. Until the latter part of the twentieth century, there was often a competitive dispute be-

Tom Cravens (21 March 1979).
Fort Worth Star-Telegram Photograph Collection
Special Collections Division
The University of Texas at Arlington Libraries

tween the M.D. and D.O. medical professionals. The osteopathic medical school was located in Fort Worth, Texas. Hooker Vandergriff and Carlisle Cravens had envisioned a joint project to bring the medical school to Arlington.

Hooker Vandergriff and Carlisle Cravens combined owned fifty acres of land in south Arlington. They had agreed with the medical college to deed the land to them if they would relocate in the city.

At the time Arlington was attracting a prominent and large contingent of M.Ds. Some did not relish having an osteopathic college in their midst, and they politically resisted the attempt to relocate it in their community.

Meanwhile, a group of osteopathic physicians in Fort Worth organized to permanently keep the college there. The Texas College of Osteopathic Medicine deeded back the land to the Vandergriffs and Cravenses. Eventually, the fifty acres reverted to the city and is now known as Cravens Park. The Texas College of Osteopathic Medicine is now part of the University of North Texas System and is one of the most prominent features of the Fort Worth community.

The City Managers

The person who becomes the manager in a council-manager type city government is critical to its operation. The manager's personality, style, and training all come into play. The stress on a city manager is great. The managerial tenure of a city manager in most cities is usually five to seven years. That is about what has occurred in Arlington during the time span covered by this study. (See Table 5.2.)

Arlington's first city manager, Albert Jones, left the office in less than a year. "His relationship with the city council was so tumultuous that the council requested his resignation. . . ."[58]

Some city managers leave deep imprints on a community. O.B. Odell became city manager when Arlington was experiencing its first growth period. Indeed, during and immediately following his tenure the population growth of the town was dramatic, increasing from 7,692 residents to 44,775, the largest percentage of growth in any decade of Arlington's history.[59]

Although he was not the first city manager, he was the first to begin to actually manage various city departments instead of simply coordinating them.[60]

He was the first city manager to serve when Tom Vandergriff became mayor. He was not a trained engineer, but began to apply sophisticated engineering applications to a city about to grow much larger. Much of the engineering expertise came from the local college then called North Texas Agricultural College, which had a fine engineering reputation. He also made use of the expertise of Lone Star Gas and Texas Electric utilities.[61]

From this engineering perspective he was able to help put together the city's first regulations for land development. With this came the city's initial building codes. Additionally, he championed the use of refunding agreements, which were already in place before he became city manager.

Most of Arlington's city managers were in office during periods of growth. And all of the city managers from O.B. Odell through Ross Calhoun served under Mayor Tom Vandergriff.

However, only one, Bill Kirchoff, was manager during a severe economic downturn. And Ross Calhoun was city manager during the completion and end of the controversial Seven Seas theme park.

Ross Calhoun had been an employee of the city of Arlington since 1963. His first employment was as director of planning. Later, he became an assistant city manager and then in 1973 became city manager. He was then thirty-two years old and one of the youngest city managers in the country. He was the last city manager to work under Mayor Tom Vandergriff.

His span of time as city manager from 1973 to 1984 was a time of great growth and development. "The city was growing so fast that it seemed like there was a different Arlington every two or three years." [62]

The city was annexing some outlying areas and there was opposition from residents who did not relish the annexation. The annexation would occur mostly to the south. The city began annexation because it felt that there was too much haphazard growth taking place in areas bordering the city.

Residents in these border areas protested that city services like water, police, and fire would not be adequately provided. A south Arlington protest group was formed for a time with the acronym: ARNO (Arlington Residents-No!). However, the annexations came about and after a while city services were made adequate.

At the same time Ross Calhoun became city manager, the city took over operation of the Seven Seas Park. The city took over the construction and operation of the park when the city and the Great Southwest Corporation, which was contracted

Arlington City Managers		
City Manager	Position Began	Position Ended
Albert Jones	January 1, 1950	August 25, 1950
O. B. Odell	November 1, 1950	December 31, 1955
William J. Pitstick	January 15, 1956	July 31, 1963
Albert W. Rollins	August 1, 1963	January 23, 1967
Herman Veselka	January 24, 1967	March 16, 1973
Ross B. Calhoun	March 16, 1973	May 3, 1984
George Campbell (Acting City Mgr)	May 4, 1984	October 1, 1984
William E. Kirchoff	October 1, 1984	February 22, 1991
George C. Campbell	February 23, 1991	January 24, 1999
Chuck Kiefer	January 25, 1999–	

Table 5.2
Arlington City Managers

to run the park, parted ways. This was hastened when the Pennsylvania Railroad, which owned a large amount of stock in Great Southwest Corporation, was hurt economically. The city then had the option of contracting with the developers of San Diego Sea Life or running the park itself. It chose the latter course.[63]

For a brief period of time, the city manager was also in part a manager of an entertainment park. After many financial difficulties, he recommended the city get out of the entertainment business. The park was then leased again, trying to make it profitable, and renamed Hawaii Kai. After a brief run under that name the park was closed completely.

Ross Calhoun, as city manager, saw the city through some tumultuous financial times. Bonds had been sold to expand the old Turnpike Stadium, renamed Arlington Stadium for the

Ross Calhoun (11 March 1984).
Fort Worth Star-Telegram Photograph Collection
Special Collections Division
The University of Texas at Arlington Libraries

new major league baseball team. Additionally, bonds had been sold to construct Seven Seas. Ross Calhoun would have to help guide the city through some financial dilemmas, especially after the demise of Seven Seas.

The city decided that the best path to financial stability was to turn the former Seven Seas location into a convention center. In the early 1980s, by a very close bond election, the citizens voted to build a convention center. Additionally, the city decided to lease some of the former theme park land to the Sheraton Hotel. The idea was to have a first-class hotel next door to a new convention center.

It was a risky idea for the city and for the city manager's office. However, the convention center and nearby hotel proved to be a success. The convention center-hotel enterprise, coupled with the continuing growth in population, averted more serious financial problems.

During Ross Calhoun's time as city manager many social problems were confronted by the city. A drug-counseling center was established. A housing authority was established to administer housing subsidies to qualified low-income families.

There was a brief controversy whether or not the city should involve itself with public housing. Some churches had proposed public housing near the intersection of Sanford and Cooper Streets. The issue was brought before the city and failed to pass after heated debate.[64]

The city manager's office recommended and attained a new city animal shelter. The old animal shelter located nearby a creek on east Sanford Street was in terrible condition. Dogs and cats were treated badly. And the methods used to euthanize the animals had been barbaric for years. "A pick-up truck exhaust was attached to an old concrete block house and gases pumped in."[65]

A new animal shelter was constructed by a bond issue and less painful euthanasia methods were employed by trained employees. This was accomplished during Ross Calhoun's term as city manager.

Much of the city manager's duties are mundane but essential. Under his administration there was a modernization of the computer system. "There was a transfer of private sector technology to the city."[66] City operations were being modernized and a higher degree of professionalism was being introduced. A new fire chief, Bill Strickland, was hired by the city manager's office from the Los Angeles Fire Department. There was discussion about a police review committee, but the idea was never implemented.

Ross Calhoun served as manager under three mayors: Vandergriff, Stovall, and Patterson. His role as city manager worked well with all of them. Even under Mayor Vandergriff's strong authority, his manager's office, he says, was always respected. "If Mayor Vandergriff wanted to speak to or contact a department head he would contact the city manager first so as not to violate the city manager's role."[67]

Ross Calhoun had worked for the city in one managerial capacity or another since 1963. On May 3, 1984, he stepped down as city manager to enter private business. George Campbell, would become acting city manager for six months until a permanent city manager could be hired.

On October 1, 1984, a new city manager, William E. "Bill" Kirchoff, was hired. He would be the first professionally trained city manager to be employed in the position with degrees in public administration.

He had been a city manager in several other communities before arriving in Arlington. As he was the first city manager to be actually trained as a city manager, he broke new political ground. And he was hired, unlike many of his predecessors, completely from outside the city, having neither been previously employed nor a resident of the city. He assumed the post following a nationwide search for a new city manager.

Bill Kirchoff was an ex-Marine with combat experience in Viet Nam. His no-nonsense managerial style would transform Arlington city government into a modern management era. Most council members who served during the time he was city manager have lauded his performance. "Bill Kirchoff as city manager was a positive turning point for the city." [68]

Even past council members who had not been on the council at the time Mr. Kirchoff was manager have reflected positively on his style. Martha Walker praises his professional style and managerial abilities. "Bill Kirchoff as city manager continued to bring professionalism to city government." [69]

However, his strong determination to implement a strict council-manager form of government did rankle some council members, notably Dick Malec. Regardless of whether Kirchoff was liked or disliked, city operations were significantly altered under his administration.

Mr. Kirchoff acknowledges that the city he came to (Arlington) had an old-time "power culture." And Ross Calhoun, his predecessor, was a good bridge between the older "power culture" and a new professional structure. [70]

He acknowledges that upon his arrival there were already good young professionals in place. He rapidly appointed others. He appointed a new police chief, David Kunkle, who also

William "Bill" Kirchoff (1 September 1984).
—*Fort Worth Star-Telegram* Photograph Collection
Special Collections Division
The University of Texas at Arlington Libraries

had a college education. The appointment of David Kunkle as police chief changed the culture of the police department to a more professional stature.[71]

Additionally, he employed many women to high-ranking city posts: Rose Jacobsen as Planning Director, Lynn Hampton as Finance Director, and Donna Brashear as Parks and Recreation director.

Mr. Kirchoff became city manager when Harold Patterson was mayor. However, he served out the rest of his stay in Arlington while Richard Greene was mayor. And "Mayor Greene was a strong political supporter of quality management." [72]

Mr. Kirchoff came into office at a time when Arlington was starting to experience, as with a good portion of the country, an economic downturn. He shifted some services to user fees. He implemented a forced reduction in some city staff.

And he implemented a "program-based budget" which allowed the council to know exactly where to place the money.[73]

William Kirchoff's goal, he says, "Was to make Arlington one of the top managed cities in the nation."[74] And by all accounts Mr. Kirchoff succeeded in that goal. Near the end of his administration the CATO Institute, a prominent national research and policy institute, ranked Arlington very high in terms of effectively run and managed cities in the country.

Mr. Kirchoff's goal of bringing in professionals to run a city goes back to his student days. He had studied how cities were managed. He had a good grasp of how the best-managed cities operated. "Even old Mayor Daley (the elder and first Mayor Richard Daley) of Chicago ran the city powerfully until his death, but he hired always the best professionals."[75]

Mr. Kirchoff resigned his city manager's post on February 22, 1991, to assume a new post as city manager of Redondo Beach, California. He left in part because of the continued arguments with council member Dick Malec over the style of a city manager form of government and its implementation.[76]

George Campbell, an assistant city manager, and also professionally trained, would be hired to fill the vacated city manager's chair.

A New Leader Emerges: Elzie Odom

In the late 1980s, Ken Groves, then a council member, approached Allan Saxe about hosting a reception for Elzie Odom. Groves wanted to know how much support there would be for Odom from the community if he ran for a city council position. A reception was held and was widely attended. In 1989, Elzie Odom would run for a seat on the city council, but would lose to Dr. Theron Brooks, a prominent local pediatrician.

Elzie Odom had arrived in Arlington in 1979 with his position as a United States postal inspector. He had served as a postal inspector for over twenty years and through his postal position had lived in many communities over the country. His job with the United States Post Office began when he served as a letter carrier in Orange, Texas. Orange is located in southeast Texas near Beaumont. "I met a lot of people as a letter carrier in Orange. Eventually I was elected to the school board there." [77]

Elzie Odom became interested in politics as a child. His father was a school board member in a small rural Texas school district. Odom grew up in a totally segregated rural Texas town.[78]

Shortly after arriving in Arlington in 1979, Elzie Odom became active in the predominately African-American Mount Olive Baptist Church. He quickly assumed a leadership role in the church. It was through Mount Olive Baptist Church that he met council member Ken Groves, who was impressed with Odom's knowledge of, and willingness to participate in, Arlington politics.

Odom's first loss to Dr. Theron Brooks in 1989 did not deter him from an interest in politics. Within one month of his election loss to Dr. Brooks, Odom was appointed to the Planning and Zoning Board with the support of Ken Groves.

In 1990 he ran again for city council against Joe Ewen and this time was elected in a very close run-off election by the slim margin of sixteen votes. This election would be a milestone for Arlington city politics.

Elzie Odom had become the first African American elected to the Arlington city council. He assumed the Place 4 seat held for many years by his friend Ken Groves, who had died earlier in the year. The following year, 1991, Joe Ewen would again run for city council and be elected.

Elzie Odom would serve as a council member until 1997, when he decided to run for mayor. He ran successfully in a very close contest, defeating fellow council member Paula Hightower. With his mayoral victory, he would again make city political history, becoming the first African American to become mayor of the city.

Elzie Odom's prominence in city politics for over a decade would pave the way for other minorities. By the end of the 1990s, minorities would play a much more significant role in a variety of city boards and commissions, like the prestigious Planning and Zoning Board and high appointed posts like police chief. And in 1993 Dan Serna would become the first Hispanic elected to the city council.

Elzie Odom (21 May 1990).
Fort Worth Star-Telegram Photograph Collection
Special Collections Division
The University of Texas at Arlington Libraries

Beginning with Martha Walker in 1972 as the first woman elected to the council, Elzie Odom, as the first African-American council member and mayor, and Dan Serna as the first Hispanic, Arlington's political landscape was now as diverse as the broader population had become.

As a council member Elzie Odom championed single-member districts and backed the eventual compromise plan adopted in 1993. He labored for the inclusion of more minorities and women on boards and commissions. And he supported the term limits placed on board and commission appointments in the 1990s.

After his election as mayor in 1997, the city named a large recreation center in the northeast sector of the town in his honor.

Chapter Six

Mavericks, Naysayers, and Watchdogs: The Conscience of a Community

Most every community of size has citizens who protest the decisions made and the way at which they were arrived. They often can disrupt the political process. They can make political leaders uncomfortable or even angry. They question, probe, write letters to the editor, appear at council meetings, lead protest groups, and even run for political office.

In turn, they often draw the ire of the decision-makers. They can be branded as naysayers, saying NO to some community projects. They can be considered as mavericks, viewing the political process a bit differently than others and often behaving or appearing as outside the mainstream. And they can be considered as watchdogs, being the eyes and ears of a citizenry too distracted or busy to concern themselves with daily political happenings. In some cases they fit the old newspaper aphorism of "comforting the afflicted, and afflicting the comfortable."

Joyce Morgan

Joyce Morgan arrived in Arlington in 1971. Her husband was with the military. She was a native of Washington, D.C. and had been active in politics all of her adult life. She viewed politics and participation as a natural and vital part of living.

Immediately after her arrival in Arlington she became active in the League of Women Voters, and remained active for nearly three decades thereafter. She became the first president of the League, and when cable television appeared in Arlington she routinely hosted a League of Women Voters program titled "Facts and Issues." There she probed, asked questions, and deliberated with nearly every elected politician and appointed city department head for many years. And in the 1970s, she was appointed to the city's Planning and Zoning Board.

For nearly three decades she attended every council meeting and the scheduled work sessions preceding the regular council meetings. The work sessions she believed helped to set the tone for the regular council meeting. This was where a consensus could be reached on many issues. She also attended various council committee meetings and some meetings of appointed boards and commissions.[1]

Joyce Morgan was a strong-willed woman always ready to discuss politics or any issue of the moment. Very often she would have a yellow, legal-size notepad and pen in one hand and a cigarette in the other.

She viewed Arlington as a town that had moved from "good ole' boy" politics from the 1950s to 1970s to a more sophisticated political architecture. "The arrival of Bill Kirchoff as city manager helped to bring professionalism to the entire city staff. This was a milestone for the city."[2]

Joyce Morgan's perception was that the older political culture of the community seldom allowed for any negative publicity to filter out about its city leaders. If there was negative publicity, as a matter of public record, about a prominent leader or family member or business associate, it seldom was reported by the local newspapers.[3]

She was critical of Arlington's lack of mass transportation for a city its size. And what she viewed as the provincial attitude of some city leaders always annoyed her. Her many years of observing Arlington politics were, on the whole, definitely favorable. The entry of more women into the political process was viewed as especially invaluable.

Her longtime and regular attendance at political happenings made her an important part of Arlington's political scene. Her permanent presence often transcended the more transient role of many office-holders. Morgan kept on top of local political issues reporting to the League and to the broader community.

Harry Robinson

Harry Robinson was intense, and though a college graduate, largely a self-educated and fearless advocate for his points of view. He was a former Marine and one could easily envision him as a Marine drill sergeant barking out commands to his troops. Occasionally, he would puff on a big cigar while discussing or arguing any number of academic or political points.

Largely coming from a libertarian perspective, he railed against any governmental intrusion in people's lives. He was critical of the city's attempts to regulate smoking, sign ordinances, and any attempt to have mass transportation.

He delighted in describing his prominent role in opposition to city attempts to join an area-wide transit system in 1979. And he equally and vociferously opposed the city's plans to form its own transit authority in 1985. However, his several attempts in campaigning for a city council place for himself were always futile.

He would frequently appear at city council meetings to speak at the end of the agenda in a period designated for citizen comments. A prolific reader, he would often quote from a variety of literary and political personalities. Even his many adversaries would admit to his command of a wide array of subjects.

His understanding of Arlington politics went far back. Both his father and uncle had been former Arlington police officers. He had held a variety of jobs in Arlington ranging from

Harry Robinson (21 March 1990).
—*Fort Worth Star-Telegram* Photograph Collection
Special Collections Division
The University of Texas at Arlington Libraries

managing a gun shop to being an automobile salesman. For a brief time he wrote a weekly column for the Arlington *Citizen-Journal*.

Robinson was a political ally of Ken Groves and avidly supported all of Groves' many campaigns and issues. He was never fearful of describing his political opponents in the most unflattering of ways. Colorful, combative, and well prepared for any debate, Robinson peppered city leaders with his criticisms and concerns for over two decades.

Lico Reyes

The owner of a theatrical company, "Parties Portable," Lico Reyes is a longtime city political observer and activist.[4] He was born in Mexico but arrived in Arlington, Texas, early in his life. He attended the University of Texas at Arlington.

Lico Reyes (10 December 1985).
—*Fort Worth Star-Telegram* Photograph Collection
Special Collections Division
The University of Texas at Arlington Libraries

As part of his theatrical company, he frequently assumed and impersonated a "Saturday Night Live" television character by the stage name of Guido Sarducci. He would often appear with his theatrical company and sing songs and make comments in an Italian dialect mimicking Father Guido Sarducci.

For many years, Reyes served on various civic organization boards, notably the Arlington Boys and Girls Club. For a time he sponsored a special Thanksgiving meal and entertainment day for underprivileged families and children. Parallel to his civic involvement was his interest in city politics. For over two decades he would attend council meetings and comment on political matters in a period devoted to any citizen concerns.

Throughout the 1980s and 1990s he systematically ran either for a council place or for mayor. In all of these attempts he would lose. He would, however, add a great deal of color and liveliness to whichever campaign he would enter as a candidate.

Like Harry Robinson, he was never afraid of tackling controversial issues nor of describing in unflattering ways those he disliked. He would champion an assortment of citizen concerns, which he believed were not addressed properly by the council. These might range from an individual citizen complaint he was aware of to broader community concerns. The Hispanic community and their welfare were of special interest.

His comic appearances as a part of his theatrical business often would interfere with his more serious political quests. Some would find it difficult to take him seriously. But underneath his love for the comedic character he would impersonate, he was a well-educated, serious political observer.

He viewed the political system as dominated by attorneys, bankers, realtors, and developers.[5] He always hoped to add a different political voice. In the spring of 2000 he again entered the race to fulfill his long held desire to become a member of the city council. He was again defeated.

Lico Reyes could be described as one of those colorful, engaging, indispensable political characters that every city in America needs.

Roy George "Skippy" Brown III

A unique tavern was operated in central Arlington for many years with the name "Skippy's Mistake." The fanciful and colorful name occasionally made one wonder just what the "mistake" was. But make no mistake about it, the proprietor of the tavern, Roy George Brown III, was an astute would-be city politician.

Mr. Brown was known to most simply as "Skippy," and he used this catchy nickname as he ventured into the political arena. As a tavern proprietor he met a lot of people over the years. He especially became acquainted with a variety of younger people, some from the university, and others from the broader community.

He would dress unconventionally for a would-be city

Skippy Brown (31 October 1986).
—*Fort Worth Star-Telegram* Photograph Collection
Special Collections Division
The University of Texas at Arlington Libraries

leader and political candidate. Typically, his attire would be a pair of jeans, colorful shirt, a ball cap, and tennis shoes. He wore his hair long and often had a cigar. However, it was exactly this unconventional lifestyle—his tavern ownership, nickname, and informal dress—which would attract a good number of Arlington citizens.

He was able to use his outsider status to good results. In 1987 he ran for city council, and his slogan became widely recognized and struck a respondent chord with many. The imaginative political slogan, "It's Everybody's Town," along with his keen knowledge of city politics, would help run a very close but losing campaign.

In the 1987 campaign he failed to make a run-off by twenty-three votes. The ensuing run-off between Grady Harris and Darrell Day was a very intense and hard fought race. Darrell Day emerged the winner.

"Skippy" Brown's principal theme was that a few people were running the city. He held that Arlington was becoming a big city, but politically resembled a small town.[6]

Buoyed by his strong 1987 showing he would run again in 1989, but again was defeated. His two campaigns, the grassroots politics, student volunteers, and many small dollar contributions added spice to the campaign seasons.

Bill Eastland

Bill Eastland was very educated, politically astute, and a professional accountant. Like Harry Robinson he primarily viewed political and economic affairs from a libertarian perspective. He not only was active and informed on city politics, but on national and international agendas as well. Coincidental with his interest in city politics was his ongoing and early activities with the Republican Party and as public school issues.

His brother, Terry Eastland, had held high-ranking positions in the United States Attorney General's Office in President Reagan's administration and later became a nationally known columnist.

Bill Eastland did run for political office. Once he ran for mayor in 1991 against Richard Greene, and later as a write-in candidate for a council place. Neither attempt was successful. He was the campaign manager for "Skippy" Brown's energetic and colorful campaign for council in 1987.

However, he made his presence felt through a variety of speaking venues, written articles, support of other candidates, and leadership roles in citizen-action groups. Newspapers would frequently seek his political perspective on controversial issues involving not only city council but public school questions as well.

He made frequent appearances before the city council to address issues of the day. His presentations were always polite but strongly worded and with confidence, laced with substantiating statistics. Eastland's training as an accountant served him well as he addressed any number of political issues involving taxation and bond propositions.

Bill Eastland (27 April 1991).
—*Fort Worth Star-Telegram* Photograph Collection
Special Collections Division
The University of Texas at Arlington Libraries

Kathy Howe

Many political activists have been drawn into city politics by what was happening or about to occur in their own neighborhoods. Zoning, apartment construction, commercial development, and special tax assessments were all likely to draw citizens into the wider political arena.

And so it was with Kathy Howe in the early 1980s when new construction and development was still spiraling. Kathy Howe lived with her husband and family in a North Arlington neighborhood. A new development was being planned nearby to which she and others objected.[7]

She came to believe that the city had zoning laws that

Kathy Howe (15 March 1985).
—*Fort Worth Star-Telegram* Photograph Collection
Special Collections Division
The University of Texas at Arlington Libraries

were too haphazard and that better and more precise guidelines were necessary. She was in opposition to the council approval of high-density apartments, especially where she resided in the north sector of the city. It was her belief that zoning procedures were too cumbersome. Further, she believed that homeowners, who were not immediately adjacent to the proposed development, were not properly notified.

Her experience in opposing development in her own neighborhood led to the belief that citizens all over the town were uneducated and unaware of the political process. She then began the attempt to share with people how local government works and how to access the political process.[8]

She became a consultant of sorts, an educator to various homeowner groups facing zoning issues. She would be called upon to volunteer her services to a multiplicity of homeowner and citizen-action groups through the 1980s.

At the same time she would begin to hold meetings in her North Arlington home with interested citizens. Persons with varied political interests and agendas would attend and present their views to those gathered.

In this way Kathy Howe had provided a place for a political assemblage and an opportunity for aspiring council members. She had a vitality similar to what Kay Taebel, and earlier Betty Fischer, had exemplified.

Eventually her informal gatherings developed into an organized political group called "Vocal." This was an acronym for: Voters Organized for Community Awareness and Leadership. It became a citywide group, with regular meetings, but minimal dues, and the publication of a newsletter.

Kathy Howe believed that the zoning decisions were mostly informally agreed upon (without any conversation between zoning board members) before any formal action on them could be taken. This was due to the pro-development posture of most planning and zoning and city council members at the time. There was nothing illegal or even unethical about this process, she holds. But it did place the average homeowner who might oppose a particular development at a disadvantage.

Kathy Howe made one attempt to be on the city council. In 1985 her principal opponent was Marti Van Ravenswaay. Van Ranvenswaay defeated Kathy Howe. Marti Van Ravenswaay for many years had been active in a variety of community efforts and had broad community and traditional leadership support. She served on the council for two terms and then was elected as a commissioner to serve on the Tarrant County Commissioners Court.

For over three decades there were many others who, for one reason or another, were in public opposition to those who held city power. There was Leo Bielinski, retired from the military and a public school teacher, who became active in opposition to city annexation.

There was Dee Turner, who would speak and write on a variety of subjects. She would be a frequent speaker at city

Mavericks, Naysayers, and Watchdogs

Dee Turner (27 April 1991).
—*Fort Worth Star-Telegram* Photograph Collection
Special Collections Division
The University of Texas at Arlington Libraries

council meetings in the period reserved for citizen comments. And her long researched essays would be distributed to select members of the community. She even ran for mayor of the city.

There was Lon Upchurch, who would be a taxpayer advocate on a variety of issues before Arlington voters. He would help to found an organization called Concerned Taxpayers of Arlington. This organization would be actively opposed to the use of tax monies for what the group considered ill-considered projects.

Bob Musgrove had been instrumental in the founding of the Arlington Museum of Art. He became known, however, for his opposition to the sales tax designated to help construct the new Ballpark in Arlington. He would write extensive newspaper articles full of financial data in order to bolster his writings.

And there was an attorney, Jim Runzheimer, who arrived

in Arlington in 1979. He opposed public funding or subsidizing of private ventures, which Arlington had occasionally done. Mr. Runzheimer, before arriving in Arlington, had worked for a city agency in Boston, Massachusetts. His perspective coming from and working for Boston city government was instructive.

Even though he was often in opposition to various Arlington city projects or leadership initiatives, he holds that Arlington during the last two decades of the century was an outstanding community. He views Arlington as a progressive and politically "clean" city. At the time he lived in Boston there was a great deal of racial and ethnic unrest. "The mayors of Arlington all fostered racial and religious harmony." [9]

His reasons for speaking out on various issues were deeply philosophical. He believed that free speech and basic liberties are important to any society, and that speaking out adds vitality to the country's freedoms.

Looking back, many former council members, mayors, and establishment leaders who were the political targets of the mavericks, naysayers, and watchdogs held similar beliefs.

Conclusion

The Political Establishment in Decline

In 1977, when Tom Vandergriff left the mayor's office, the old establishment that had held together and governed so well and so long lost its leader. But it did not fall apart all at once. Strong leaders like Richard Greene were able and willing to guide the city through some troublesome times. In essence, Greene preserved the Vandergriff legacy.

But by the mid-1980s, the broader establishment—composed of developers, bankers, real estate brokers, newspapers, and old time families—would begin to lessen its grip on the community. Those whose names and faces would be instantly recognizable and politically potent would begin to fade.

The mid-1980s to the early 1990s was an era of collapsing oil prices, defunct banks, savings and loans, and federal takeover of much commercial and residential property. Local control of many financial institutions had been transferred to outside interests.

For years, land and its attendant zoning was at the heart of Arlington's elite wealth. By the end of the 1990s, much of Arlington's land area had been zoned and developed. The local elites would no longer be so captivated by land use. And the growing global technological changes would also alter the ways in which wealth was accumulated. The actions of a city council would not be as important as before to economic fortune.

Before the end of the twentieth century, the influential newspaper, Arlington *Citizen-Journal*, ceased publication. Earlier it had been purchased by the *Fort Worth Star-Telegram*, and for a while retained its name. The *Star-Telegram* had been purchased by Capital Cities Corporation, which in turn was purchased by Disney Corporation. Disney eventually sold it to Knight-Ridder Corporation. The longtime local control of an important media outlet had been transferred to outside interests.

By the end of the 1990s decade, Belo Corporation, which in prior years had owned and operated a newspaper in the community, had started another newspaper, the *Arlington Morning News*. This new media addition would add to the competition and coverage of the political scene. Neither the *Star-Telegram* nor the *Arlington Morning News* would be reluctant about coverage of any aspect of a public official, private or public.

Dramatic changes in the political structure and process were inaugurated. The election of some city council members by single-member districts, resisted so long by local elites, finally came about. This made it more difficult for the older elites to maintain authority.

In past years political campaigns were run by scores of volunteers at phone banks or over a dining room table folding campaign pamphlets. Increasingly, by the 1990s campaigns were being managed by professionals.

The earlier adoption by the state legislature of an Open Meetings Act and an Open Records Act allowed citizens and the media more access to decision-making. Neighborhood groups, which had for years struggled against various zoning and annexation decisions, became more viable and cohesive.

The important and heralded growth of the city brought about major changes. Ironically, the pro-growth initiatives that the establishment had always favored helped to bring about the establishment's demise. As the city's population grew, people arrived from all parts of the country and the world. They brought with them new political perspectives and vitality as well as problems, which the city had never before faced. And many newcomers neither recognized nor showed obeisance to those who had managed and led Arlington in the past.

The old families, which had held power for so long, began to grow old. The patriarchs and matriarchs of Arlington began to fade. Some of their offspring had interests outside of the community in which they were born. Most were disinterested in the political power once held by their families.

The changes in Arlington's political environment are not peculiar to this city. Similar political alterations have occurred in Dallas, Fort Worth, and surrounding cities.

There will always be local elites. There will always be a few who have more power than others. But the old cohesiveness, consensus building, and political longevity of its elected and appointed officials have been substantially altered.

Reunion of former mayors, council members, and city managers (March 1995).
—Photo courtesy of Martha Walker

Appendix A

Interviews

Name	Date
R.G. "Wick" Alexander	21 November 1995
Tony Arangio	13 February 1997
Les Blaser	6 January 1997
Carma Borth	15 January 1997
Roy George "Skippy" Brown III	11 February 1997
Ross Calhoun	15 June 1996
O.K. Carter	12 January 1996
Tom Cravens	3 November 1995
James Cribbs	1 March 1996
Ginger Vandergriff Deering	5 February 1997
Gary Dworkin	26 February 1996
Bill Eastland	20 May 2000
Bryan Eppstein	6 June 2000
Jewell Fox	15 March 1988
Betty and Nile Fischer	4 June 1996
Dan Gould, Jr.	2 June 2000 & 19 January 2001
Kenneth Groves	5 April 1986
Richard Greene	21 June 1996
Sam Hamlett	10 February 1997
George Hawkes	2 December 1995
Kelly Jones	7 January 1998

James "Big Daddy" Knapp	12 May 1980
Bill Kirchoff	17 December 1996
Dottie Lynn	26 January 1996
Dick Malec	12 February 1997
James Martin	6 January 1996
Joyce Morgan	5 July 1996
Jim Norwood	18 December 1996
Elzie Odom	29 December 1997
Penny Patrick	9 June 2000
Harold Patterson	2 January 1996
Rena Pederson	11 February 1997
Paula Hightower Pierson	17 December 1997
Jeanette Groves Proctor	20 March 1996
Lico Reyes	7 February 1997
Maxine Roane	29 September 1995
Jim Runzheimer	8 June 2000
Ralph Shelton	27 October 1995
S.J. Stovall	5 December 1995
Kay Taebel	25 November 1995
Barton Thompson	9 October 1995
Tom J. Vandergriff	30 December 1996
Marti Van Ravenswaay	29 January 1997
Herman Veselka	7 January 2000
Martha Walker	12 October 1995
Roger "Rocky" Walton	4 January 1998
Howard Wilemon	10 February 1997
Kathy (Howe) Winslow	23 January 1997
Paul Yarbrough	4 April 1972

Appendix B

ARLINGTON MAYORS

1880 C.D. King
1881 M. J. Brinson
1882
1883
1884 George W. Finger
1885 E. E. Rankin
1885 Robert George
1886 George W. Finger
1887
1888
1889 M. J. Brinson
1890
1891 Willis Timmerman
1892 N. K. Grove
1893 Willis Timmerman
1894
1895
1896
1897
1898
1899 C. D. King
1900 W. C. Weeks
1901
1902 T. B. Collins
1903

1904 T. G. Bailey
1905
1906 W. C. Weeks (resigned 1909)
1907
1908
1909 J. P. Fielder (3 months)
1909 Dr. W. H. Davis
1910 A. C. Barnes
1911
1912 Dr. R. H. Greer
1913
1914 P. F. McKee
1915 Dr. R. H. Greer
1916
1917
1918
1919 W. H. Rose
1920
1921
1922
1923 W. H. Rose (died 1923)
1923 W. G. Hiett
1924
1925 Hugh M. Moore
1926 Elmer L. Taylor

151

1927 W. G. Hiett	1964
1928	1965
1929	1966
1930	1967
1931 John H. Pilant	1968
1932	1969
1933 W. L. Barret	1970
1934	1971
1935 W. F. Altman	1972
1936	1973
1937	1974
1938	1975
1939	1976
1940	1977 Tom J. Vandergriff
1941	(resigned)
1942	1977 S. J. Stovall (appointed)
1943	1978 S. J. Stovall
1944	1979
1945	1980
1946	1981
1947 B. C. Barnes	1982
1948	1983 Harold E. Patterson
1949	1984
1950	1985
1951 Tom J. Vandergriff	1986
1952	1987 Richard E. Greene
1953	1988
1954	1989
1955	1990
1956	1991
1957	1992
1958	1993
1959	1994
1960	1995
1961	1996
1962	1997 Elzie D. Odom
1963	

(Courtesy of City Secretary's Office, Arlington, Texas)

Appendix C

Arlington Mayors from 1884 to 2000

NAME	TERM OF OFFICE
Altman, W. F	April 2, 1935–April 1, 1947
Bailey, T. G.	April 14, 1904–April 12, 1906
Barnes, A. C.	April 10, 1910–April 11, 1912
Barnes, B.C.	April 1, 1947–April 3, 1951
Barrett, W. L.	April 4, 1933–April 2, 1935
Brinson, M. J.	1881–1884
	December 10, 1889–July 14, 1891
Collins, T. B.	April 10, 1902–April 14, 1904
Davis, Dr. W. H.	April 8, 1909–April 10, 1910
Fielder, J. P.	February 11, 1909–April 8, 1909
Finger, George W.	April 15, 1884–March 10, 1885
	March 9, 1886–December 10, 1889
George, Robert	April 28, 1885–March 9, 1886
Greer, Dr. R. H.	April 11, 1912–April 11, 1914
	April 9, 1915–October 1, 1919
Greene, Richard E.	April 4, 1987–May 6, 1997
Grove, N. K.	May 10, 1892–September 12, 1893
Hiett, W. G.	May 19, 1923–April 7, 1925
	April 11, 1927–April 21, 1931
King, C. D.	1880–1881
	January 10, 1899–March 8, 1900
Moore, Hugh M.	April 7, 1925–May 3, 1926
McKee, P. F	April 11, 1914–April 9, 1915
Odom, Elzie D.	May 6, 1997 -
Patterson, Harold E.	April 12, 1983–April 4, 1987
Pilant, John H.	April 21, 1931–April 4, 1933
Rankin, E. E.	March 10, 1885–April 28, 1885

Rose, W. H.	October 1, 1919–May 16, 1923 (died)
Stovall, S. J.	January 18, 1977–April 12, 1983
Taylor, Elmer L.	May 3, 1926–April 11, 1927
Timmerman, Willis	July 14, 1891–May 10, 1892
	September 12, 1893–January 10, 1899
Vandergriff, Tom J.	April 3, 1951–January 11, 1977
Weeks, W. C.	March 8, 1900–April 10, 1902
	April 12, 1906–February 11, 1909

[Terms of office (months and days) may vary due to use of elections, canvassing of vote totals, or swearing-in, as the official dates by records of the City Secretary's Office.]

(Courtesy of City Secretary's Office, Arlington, Texas)

Appendix D

CITY COUNCIL
October 1919 to May 2000

ALEXANDER, R. G. (Wick)	April 6, 1971–April 12, 1977
ALTMAN, W. F.	April 3, 1934–April 2, 1935
ATKINS, ELMER	April 1, 1947–April 5, 1949
BALL, JOHN R., JR	April 7, 1964–April 7, 1970
BARBER, J. W	April 7, 1925–April 5, 1927
BARNES, BARNEY C.	April 7, 1942–April 4, 1944
BATES, F. J.	April 5, 1932–April 3, 1934
BEASLEY, C. L.	April 7, 1936–April 4, 1944
BERMAN, LEO	April 17, 1979–April 30, 1985
BLACKMAN, D. E	October 1, 1919–September 3, 1921
BLAIR, W. G.	April 4, 1944–April 6, 1948
BROOKS, THERON E. III	May 6, 1989–May 29, 1993
BROWN, CHARLES E. C.	April 2, 1963–July 3, 1970
BRUNER, GARY W	April 4, 1981–April 6, 1985
BRUNER, JOE (District 1)	May 20, 2000–
BUCHANAN, M. D.	July 12, 1960–April 12, 1966
BURGEN, JULIA (District 5)	May 3, 1997–
CAPEHART, SHERI (District 2)	May 6, 2000–
CARROLL, CLEM B.	April 13, 1982–May 1, 1984
CLUCK, ROBERT N. (District 4)	May 1, 1999–
COBLE, WAYNE A.	April 3, 1976–April 1, 1978
COOPER, H. W.	April 4, 1944–April 2, 1946
CRIPPEN, JACK	April 2, 1963–April 4, 1967
DALBY, M. C.	April 2, 1946–April 6, 1948
DAVIS, C. H.	April 3, 1923–April 7, 1925
	April 11, 1927–April 3, 1928
DAY, DARRELL	April 18, 1987–May 7, 1988

DEAHL, CHARLES J.	April 14, 1981–April 17, 1984
DITTO, MIKE W., JR.	April 6, 1948–April 1, 1952
DUNCAN, MAURICE E.	April 1, 1952–April 3, 1956
DUNSWORTH, H.A.D.	April 7, 1953–April 2, 1963
ECHOLS, WALKER M.	April 3, 1928–April 1, 1930
	April 2, 1935–April 1, 1947
EDWARDS, MARION W.	June 18, 1946–April 3, 1947
ELDER, JOSEPH E., JR.	April 1, 1947–April 3, 1951
EWEN, JOE	May 4, 1991–May 1, 1999
FAULKNER, J. D.	April 6, 1926–April 11, 1927
FOSTER, CLARENCE R.	April 1, 1952–April 1, 1958
GEE, JOHN S.	April 5, 1949–April 7, 1953
GREEN, FORREST	April 2, 1940–April 7, 1942
GREENE, RICHARD E.	April 7, 1984–January 27, 1987
Mayor	April 4, 1987–May 3, 1997
GRIMMETT, O. C.	April 1, 1930–April 3, 1934
GROVES, KENNETH	April 1, 1978–March 3, 1981 (Place 4)
	September 7,1982–April 2,1983 (Place 1
	April 7, 1984–January 16,1990 (Place 4)
	Died–January 16, 1990
HAMLETT, SAM	May 10, 1977–May 1, 1979
HIETT, W G	October 1, 1919–May 19, 1923
HIGHTOWER, D. D.	April 10, 1920–April 10, 1922
HIGHTOWER, PAULA	May 6, 1989–May 3, 1997
HOLMAN, DIXON H. (Father)	April 2, 1977–November 3, 1981
HOLMAN, DIXON R. (Son) (District 6-1994)	May 2, 1992–
	May 20, 2000
HOUSTON, J. M.	April 7, 1925–April 5, 1927
ISAACS, SAM C.	April 3, 1934–April 2, 1940
JAMES, E M.	April 1, 1924–April 6, 1926
JONES, L. KELLY	April 20, 1985–May 6, 1989
KIER, JAMES M.	April 4, 1981–April 7, 1984
KNAPP, WILLIAM	March 20, 1924–April 7, 1925
LUTTRELL, GEORGE E.	April 10, 1922–September 15, 1924
LYNN, DOTTIE (District 7—1994)	April 3, 1982–January 27, 1987
	May, 1988–May 20, 2000
MALEC, RICHARD (DICK)	April 5, 1986–May 12, 1992
MANER, DOLAND C.	April 4, 1967–May 6, 1975
McCARTER, R T.	April 7, 1931–April 2, 1935
McCOLLUM, STEVE (District 6)	May 20, 2000–
McFADIN, BILL	May 16, 1989–May 29, 1993
McKNIGHT, RAY	September 15, 1924–April 13, 1925

MEBUS, ROBERT L. (JERRY)	April 1, 1958–April 7, 1964
MORGAN, L. S.	April 7, 1931–April 2, 1935
NASH BARBARA (District 1)	May 17, 1997–May 20, 2000
NICHOLS, H. M.	April 3, 1928–April 1, 1930
NORWOOD, JIM	May 1, 1984–April 5, 1986
ODOM ELZIE D. (District 1—1994)	May 9, 1990–May 3, 1997
Mayor	May 3, 1997–
OGLE, WAYNE (District 3)	May 6, 1995–
PATTERSON HAROLD E.	April 5, 1966–April 2, 1983
Mayor	April 2, 1983–April 4, 1987
PHILLIPS DAN	April 6, 1985–May 16, 1989
PILANT JOHN H.	April 1, 1930–April 7, 1931
PURVIS, DIXON H.	April 5, 1955–April 2, 1963
REMINGTON, PAT (District 8)	May 3 1997–
ROSS CECIL	April 3, 1956–April 1, 1958
RUPAY, JUDY M. (District 2)	May 7, 1994–May 6, 2000
SERNA, DAN T. (District 8)	May 29, 1993–May 3, 1997
SHELTON, RALPH B.	April 11, 1972–April 6, 1976
SLAUGHTER, HOMER	March 31, 1922–April 1, 1924
SNIDER, CAROLYN W.	May 3, 1975–June 17, 1982
Died	June 17, 1982
SNIDER, RICHARD A.	April 6, 1948–April 1, 1952
SNIDER, WILLIAM W.	April 2, 1983–May 4, 1991
STOVALL, S. J.	April 7, 1964–January 11, 1977

As Mayor Pro Tempore, became Acting Mayor on January 12, 1977, when Vandergriff resigned.

Mayor	April 2, 1977–April 2, 1983
SUTTON, WILLARD C.	April 7, 1964–April 4, 1972
TAEBEL, KAY	May 29, 1993–May 6, 1995
TAYLOR, ELMER	April 6, 1926–May 4, 1926
THOMPSON, BARTON	April 7, 1970–May 9, 1972
TURCK, WILL	May 6, 1926–April 11, 1927
VANRAVENSWAAY, MARTI	April 6, 1985–May 6, 1989
VINSON, C. C.	March 17, 1922–April 9, 1923
WALKER, MARTHA	May 16, 1972–April 3, 1982
WALLACE, D. H.	September 9, 1921–April 10, 1922
WALLACE, FRANK	July 12, 1960–April 2, 1963
WALTHER, LARRY	April 4, 1987–May 5, 1990
WALTON, ROGER (ROCKY)	May 5, 1990–May 7, 1994
WHARTON, PAUL C.	November 24, 1981–April 6, 1985
WALDROP, TOM C.	April 1, 1958–April 7, 1964
WEBB, T. C.	April 5, 1927–April 7, 1931

WILEY, S. A.	April 5, 1927–April 7, 1931
WOLFE, MARTIN D.	April 3, 1951–April 5, 1955
WRIGHT, J. R.	April 10, 1920–April 6, 1922
	May 19, 1923–March 20, 1924
	April 11, 1927–April 3, 1928
WRIGHT, RON (District 7)	May 20, 2000–

(Courtesy of City Secretary's Office, Arlington, Texas)

Appendix E

30 Years of City Elections, Arlington Texas

Date	Vote Totals	Type Of Election
5-02-98	16,350	Council, Sales Tax
5-17-97	2,222	Council Runoff
5-03-97	17,528	Council
1-18-97	6,676	Park Bond
5-04-96	3,765	Council, Charter
5-06-95	11,324	Council
5-07-94	7,807	Council
1-15-94	5,118	Bond
11-02-93	8,522	Charter, Single-Member Districts
5-29-93	24,531	Council Runoff
5-01-93	36,073	Council
1-16-93	5,614	Library Bond
5-02-92	9,119	Council
5-04-91	15,477	Council, Bond Civil Service
1-19-91	33,860	Sales Tax Ballpark
8-11-90	11,024	Charter, Single-Member Districts
5-19-90	5,140	Runoff (Odom v. Ewen)
5-05-90	8,451	Council
5-06-89	9,898	Council
8-13-88	9,352	Bond
5-07-88	7,822	Council, Charter
4-18-87	5,511	Runoff (Day v. Harris)

Date	Votes	Issue
4-04-87	18,431	Council
4-05-86	13,122	Council, Charter
8-10-85	10,244	Transit Authority
4-20-85	4,223	Runoff (Jones v. Kinnard)
4-06-85	14,480	Council
2-02-85	8,478	Bond
4-21-84	4,140	Runoff (Norwood v. Kinnard)
4-07-84	8,261	Council, Charter
4-02-83	10,063	Council
8-28-82	5,830	Runoff (Snider v. Groves)
8-14-82	6,131	Bingo/Special Council
4-03-82	11,914	Council, Charter
11-17-81	2,218	Runoff (Wharton v. Barnett)
11-03-81	4,930	Special (Holman Resigned)
4-04-81	12,651	Council
12-06-80	8,399	Bond
4-05-80	5,418	Council, Charter
1-12-80	2,028	Bond
4-21-79	7,201	Runoff (Berman v. Hamlett)
4-07-79	13,419	Council, Civil Service, Single-Member Districts
4-01-78	4,246	Council
10-25-77	5,156	Bond
5-10-77	2,464	Runoff (Hamlett v. Wolfe)
4-02-77	5,719	Council
4-03-76	2,485	Council
5-06-75	6,196	Runoff (Snider v. Saxe)
4-01-75	8,659	Council
4-02-74	784	Council
4-03-73	2,034	Council
4-04-72	7,989	Council
4-06-71	8,258	Council
4-07-70	2,795	Council
4-01-69	1,548	Council
4-02-68	3,100	Council

(Courtesy of City Secretary's Office, Arlington, Texas)

Appendix F

Arlington Mayors & Commissioners, 1921–1956

APRIL 5, 1921
W. H. Rose, Mayor
W. G. Hiett, Commissioner
D. E. Blackburn, Commissioner

APRIL 4, 1922
C. C. Vinson, Commissioner
Homer Slaughter, Commissioner

APRIL 3, 1923
W. H. Rose, Mayor
W. G. Hiett, Commissioner
C. H. Davis, Commissioner

APRIL 1, 1924
George E. Luttrell, Commissioner
E. M. James, Commissioner

APRIL 7, 1925
Hugh M. Moore, Mayor
J. W. Barber, Commissioner
J. M. Houston, Commissioner

APRIL 6, 1926
J. D. Faulkner, Commissioner
Elmer Taylor, Commissioner

APRIL 5, 1927
W. G. Hiett, Mayor
T. C. Webb, Commissioner
S. A. Wiley, Commissioner

APRIL 3, 1928
H. M. Nichols, Commissioner
Walker Echols, Commissioner

APRIL 2, 1929
W. G. Hiett, Mayor
T. C. Webb, Commissioner
S. A. Wiley, Commissioner

APRIL 1, 1930
John H. Pilant, Commissioner
O. C. Grimmett, Commissioner

APRIL 7, 1931
John H. Pilant, Mayor
L. S. Borgan, Commissioner
R. T. McCarter, Commissioner

APRIL 5, 1932
O. C. Grimmett, Commissioner
F. J. Bates, Commissioner

APRIL 4, 1933
W. L. Barrett, Mayor
L. S. Morgan, Commissioner
R. T. McCarter, Commissioner

APRIL 3, 1934
W. F. Altman, Commissioner
Sam C. Isaacs, Commissioner

APRIL 2, 1935
W. F. Altman, Mayor
Walker Echols, Commissioner
Homer Slaughter, Commissioner

APRIL 7, 1936
Sam C. Isaacs, Commissioner
C. L. Beasley, Commissioner

APRIL 6, 1937
W. F. Altman, Mayor
Walker Echols, Commissioner
Homer Slaughter, Commissioner

APRIL 19, 1938
C. L. Beasley, Commissioner
Sam C. Isaacs, Commissioner

APRIL 4, 1939
W. F. Altman, Mayor
Homer Slaugher, Commissioner
Walker Echols, Commissioner

APRIL 2, 1940
C. L. Beasley, Commissioner
Forrest Green, Commissioner

APRIL 1, 1941
W. F. Altman, Mayor
Walker Echols, Commissioner
Homer Slaughter, Commissioner

APRIL 7, 1942
Barney C. Barnes, Commissioner
C. L. Beasley, Commissioner

APRIL 6, 1943
W. F. Altman, Mayor
Walker Echols, Commissioner
Homer Slaughter, Commissioner

APRIL 4, 1944
W. G. Blair, Commissioner
H. W. Cooper, Commissioner

APRIL 3, 1945
W. F. Altman, Mayor
Walker Echols, Commissioner
Homer Slaughter, Commissioner

APRIL 2, 1946
W. G. Blair, Commissioner
M. C. Dalby, Commissioner

APRIL 1, 1947
B. C. Barnes, Mayor
Joseph Elder, Jr., Commissioner
Elmer Atkins, Commissioner

APRIL 6, 1948
Mike W. Ditto, Jr., Commissioner
Richard A. Snider, Commissioner

APRIL 5, 1949
B. C. Barnes, Mayor
Joseph H. Elder, Jr., Commissioner
John S. Gee, Commissioner

APRIL 5, 1950
Richard A. Snider, Commissioner
Mike W. Ditto, Commissioner

Appendices

APRIL 3, 1951
Tom J. Vandergriff, Mayor
Martin D. Wolfe, Commissioner
John S. Gee, Commissioner

APRIL 1, 1952
Clarence R. Foster,
 Commissioner
Maurice E. Duncan,
 Commissioner

APRIL 7, 1953
Tom J. Vandergriff, Mayor
H.A.D. Dunsworth,
 Commissioner
Martin D. Wolfe, Commissioner

APRIL 6, 1954
Maurice E. Duncan,
 Commissioner
Clarence R. Foster,
 Commissioner

APRIL 5, 1955
Tom J. Vandergriff, Mayor
H.A.D. Dunsworth,
 Commissioner
Dixon H. Purvis, Commissioner

APRIL 3, 1956
Clarence R. Foster,
 Commissioner
Cecil C. Ross, Commissioner

(Courtesy of City Secretary's Office, Arlington, Texas)

Appendix G

Arlington Elected Officials & Election Results
1957–2000

APRIL 2, 1957
Tom J. Vandergriff, Mayor	3,563
H.A.D. Dunsworth, Commissioner	1,471
Dixon H. Purvis, Commissioner	1,483

APRIL 1, 1958
Robert L. Mebus, Commissioner	926
Tom C. Waldrop, Commissioner	860

APRIL 7, 1959
Tom J. Vandergriff, Mayor	1,140
H.A.D. Dunsworth, Commissioner	812
Dixon H. Purvis, Commissioner	669

APRIL 5, 1960
Robert L. Mebus, Commissioner	797
Tom C. Waldrop, Commissioner	809

JULY 12, 1960 First Election after City Charter Revision
Frank Wallace, Councilman, Place 3	991
M. D. Buchanan, Councilman Place 6	1,431

APRIL 4, 1961
Tom J. Vandergriff, Mayor	5,258
H.A.D. Dunsworth, Councilman, Place 1	2,655
Dixon H. Purvis, Councilman, Place 2	2,840
Frank Wallace, Councilman, Place 3	5,198

APRIL 3, 1962
Robert L. Mebus, Councilman, Place 4	1,781
Tom C. Waldrop, Councilman, Place 5	944
M. D. Buchanan, Councilman, Place 6	1,217

APRIL 2, 1963
Tom J. Vandergriff, Mayor	3,019
Jack Crippen, Councilman, Place 1	1,678
S. J. Stovall, Councilman, Place 2	1,866
Charles E. C. Brown, Councilman, Place 3	2,083

APRIL 7, 1964
Willard C. Sutton, Councilman, Place 4	1,687
John R. Ball, Jr., Councilman, Place 5	1,349
M. D. Buchanan, Councilman, Place 6	2,890

APRIL 6, 1965
Tom J. Vandergriff, Mayor	1,948
Jack Crippen, Councilman, Place 1	1,017
S. J. Stovall, Councilman, Place 2	2,096
Charles E.C.Brown, Councilman, Place 3	2,082

APRIL 5, 1966
Willard C. Sutton, Councilman, Place 4	1,989
John R. Ball, Jr., Councilman, Place 5	1,137
Harold E.Patterson, Councilman, Place 6	1,789

APRIL 4, 1967
Tom J. Vandergriff, Mayor	2,446
Doland C. Maner, Councilman, Place 1	1,492
S. J. Stovall, Councilman, Place 2	2,090
Charles E.C. Brown, Councilman, Place 3	1,876

APRIL 2, 1968
Willard C. Sutton, Councilman, Place 4	2,803
John R. Ball, Jr., Councilman, Place 5	2,372
Harold E. Patterson, Councilman, Place 6	2,823

APRIL 1, 1969
Tom J. Vandergriff, Mayor	1,429
Doland C. Maner, Councilman, Place 1	1,366
S. J. Stovall, Councilman, Place 2	1,390

Charles E. C. Brown, Councilman, Place 3 — 1,038

APRIL 7, 1970
Willard C. Sutton, Councilman, Place 4 — 1,922
Barton Thompson, Councilman, Place 5 — 1,774
Harold E. Patterson, Councilman, Place 6 — 2,478

APRIL 6, 1971
Tom J. Vandergriff, Mayor — 6,859
Doland C. Maner, Councilman, Place 1 — 5,576
S. J. Stovall, Councilman, Place 2 — 6,607
R. G. Alexander, Councilman, Place 3 — 3,354

APRIL 4, 1972
Ralph B. Shelton, II, Council, Place 4 — 3,993
Barton Thompson, Council, Place 5 (In runoff) — 3,313
Martha Walker, Council, Place 5 (In runoff) — 3,283
Harold E. Patterson, Council, Place 6 — 5,896

MAY 9, 1972 Runoff
Martha Walker, winner, Place 5 — 2,139
Barton Thompson, — 1,997

APRIL 3, 1973
Tom J. Vandergriff, Mayor — 2,034
Doland C. Maner, Council, Place 1 — 1,621
S. J. Stovall, Council, Place 2 — 1,735
R. G. (Wick) Alexander, Council, Place 3 — 2,046

APRIL 2, 1974
Ralph B. Shelton, Council, Place 4 — 638
Martha Walker, Council, Place 5 — 651
Harold E. Patterson, Council, Place 6 — 654

APRIL 1, 1975
Tom J. Vandergriff, Mayor — 6,094
S. J. Stovall, Council, Place 2 — 4,211
R. G. Alexander, Council, Place 3 — 6,099

MAY 6, 1975 Runoff
Carolyn W. Snider, winner, Place 1 — 3,406
Allan Saxe — 2,790

Appendices 167

APRIL 3, 1976
Wayne Coble, Council, Place 4	2,485
Martha Walker, Council, Place 5	2,494
Harold E. Patterson, Council Place 6	1,818

JANUARY 11, 1977
Tom J. Vandergriff resigned as Mayor

JANUARY 18, 1977
S. J. Stovall appointed to be Mayor by Council

APRIL 2, 1977
S. J. Stovall, Mayor	4,353
Carolyn W. Snider, Council, Place 1	4,003
Dixon Holman, Council, Place 2	3,191

MAY 10, 1977 Runoff
Sam Hamlett, winner, Council, Place 3	1,587
Don J. Wolfe	877

APRIL 1 1978
Ken Groves, Council, Place 4	2,162
Martha Walker, Council, Place 5	3,348
Harold E. Patterson, Council, Place 6	2,539

APRIL 7, 1979
S. J. Stoval, Mayor	9,710
Carolyn W. Snider, Council, Place 1	8,602
Dixon Holman Council, Place 2	8,282

APRIL 21 1979 Runoff
Leo Berman, winner, Council, Place 3	3,707
Sam Hamlett	3,494

APRIL 5, 1980
Ken Groves, Council, Place 4	4,037
Martha Walker, Council, Place 5	3,699
Harold Patterson, Council, Place 6	2,821

MARCH 3, 1981
Ken Groves resigned Council, Place 4

APRIL 4, 1981 First Election after Charter Revision (Larger Council)

S. J. Stovall, Mayor	7,899
Carolyn W. Snider, Council, Place 1	8,416
Dixon Holman, Council, Place 2	8,449
Leo Berman, Council, Place 3	8,142
Charles J. Deahl, Council, Place 4	7,151
James M. Kier, Council, Place 7 (new)	7,859
Gary W. Bruner, Council, Place 8 (new)	5,873

NOVEMBER 3 1981
Election to Fill Dixon Holman's. Place 2 seat (he resigned)

NOVEMBER 17 1981 Runoff to Fill Place 2

Paul C. Wharton, winner, Place 2	1,189
Joe Barnett	1,029

APRIL 3, 1982

Charles J. Deahl, Council, Place 4	6,382
Dottie Lynn, Council, Place 5	6,016

APRIL 3, 1982

Clem B. Carroll, Council, Place 6	8,428
James Kier, Council, Place 7	6,371

JUNE 17, 1982
Death of Carolyn W. Snider, Council, Place 1

AUGUST 14, 1982 Election to fill Place 1

Bill Snider	2,991
Ken Groves	2,387

AUGUST 28, 1982 Runoff

Ken Groves, winner, Place 1	3,105
Bill Snider	2,725

APRIL 2, 1983

Harold E. Pattterson, Mayor	8,816
Bill Snider, Council, Place 1	5,098
Paul C. Wharton, Council, Place 2	4,740
Leo Berman, Council, Place 3	7,487
Gary W. Bruner, Council, Place 8	7,614

APRIL 7, 1984
Ken Groves, Council, Place 4	6,051
Dottie Lynn, Council, Place 5	6,625
Richard Greene, Council, Place 7	6,424

APRIL 21, 1984 Runoff
Jim Norwood, winner, Council, Place 6	2,345
Jake Kinnard	1,795

APRIL 6, 1985
Harold E. Patterson, Mayor	8,696
William W. Snider, Council, Place 1	6,877
Marti VanRayenswaay, Council, Place 2	7,633
Dan Phillips, Council, Place 8	8,647

APRIL 20, 1985 Runoff
Kelly Jones, Council, Place 3	2,253
Jake Kinnard	1,970

APRIL 5, 1986
Ken Groves, Council, Place 4	9,205
Dottie Lynn, Council, Place 5	8,972

APRIL 5, 1986
Dick Malec, Council, Place 6	6,806
Richard Greene, Council, Place 7	9,527

APRIL 4, 1987
Richard Greene, Mayor	10,676
William W. Snider, Council, Place 1	13,301
Marti VanRavenswaay, Council, Place 2	13,306
Kelly Jones, Council, Place 3	9,443
Larry Walther, Council, Place 7	5,594
Dan Phillips, Council, Place 8	13,219

APRIL 18, 1987 Runoff
Darrell Day, winner, Council, Place 5	3,885
Grady Harris	1,686

Note: State changed General Election date to the first Saturday in May because of State Primary Elections now in March.

MAY 7, 1988
Ken Groves, Council, Place 4	4,990
Dottie Lynn, Council, Place 5	4,023
Dick Malec, Council, Place 6	5,103
Larry Walther, Council, Place 7	NA

MAY 6, 1989
Richard Greene, Mayor	8,713
William W. Snider, Council, Place 1	7,018
Theron E. Brooks, III, Place 2	6,199
Bill McFadin, Council, Place 3	5,133
Paula Hightower, Council, Place.8	6,275

MAY 5, 1990
Dottie Lynn, Council, Place 5	6,164
Dick Malec, Council, Place 6	5,655
Roger "Rocky" Walton, Council, Place 7	4,079

MAY 19, 1990 Runoff
Elzie Odom, winner, Council, Place 4	2,578
Joe Ewen	2,562

MAY 4, 1991
Richard E. Greene, Mayor	10,908 (73%)
Joe Ewen, Council, Place 1	8,934 (66%)
Theron E. Brooks, III, Place 2	9,547 (71%)

MAY 4, 1991
Bill McFadin, Council, Place 3	10,090 (100%)
Paula Hightower, Council, Place 8	8,361 (59%)

MAY 2, 1992
Elzie D. Odom, Council, Place 4	5,846 (67%)
Dottie Lynn, Council, Place 5	5,811 (67%)
Dixon R. Holman, Council, Place 6	5,254 (60%)
Roger "Rocky" Walton, Council, Place 7	4,889 (58%)

MAY 1, 1993
Richard E. Greene, Mayor	27,951 (93%)
Joe Ewen, Council, Place 1	16,892 (59%)
Paula Hightower, Council, Place 8	20,509 (66%)

MAY 29, 1993 Runoff
Dan Serna, winner, Council, Place 3,   12,475
Kay Taebel, Council, Place 2   12,178

Note: Single Member Districts were approved by Election held November 2, 1993

MAY 7, 1994
Elzie Odom, District 1   1,233 (66.22%)
Judy M. Rupay, District 2   935 (51.06%)
Dixon R. Holman, District 6 (At Large)   3,816 (52.22%)
Dottie Lynn, District 7 (At Large)   5,284 (72.51%)

MAY 6, 1995
Richard E. Greene, Mayor   7,959 (72%)
Wayne Ogle, District 3   829 (52%)
Joe Ewen, District 4   2,009 (62%)
Paula Hightower, District 5   1,435 (87%)
Dan T. Serna, District 8 (At Large)   5,839 (53%)

MAY 4, 1996
Elzie Odom, District 1   602 (100%)
Judy M. Rupay, District 2   744 (81.40%)
Dixon R. Holman, District 6   2,728 (100%)
Dottie Lynn, District 7   2,510 (69.88%)

MAY 3, 1997
Elzie Odom, Mayor   7,060 (50.19%)
Wayne Ogle, District 3   1,330 (69.82%)
Joe Ewen, District 4   3,100 (70.25%)
Julia Burgen, District 5   1,757 (50.52%)
Pat Remington, District 8   11,480 (82.38%)

MAY 17, 1997 Runoff
Barbara Nash, District 1 (Unexpired Term)   1,394 (62.74%)

MAY 2, 1998
Barbara Nash, District 1   1,632 (50.48%)
Judy M. Rupay, District 2   2,485 (100%)
Dixon R. Holman, District 6   7,997 (55.52%)
Dottie Lynn, District 7   8,154 (54.43%)

MAY 1, 1999
Elzie Odom, Mayor   6,290 (77.29%)
Wayne Ogle, District 3   644 (78.73%)
Robert N. Cluck, District 4   1,483 (50.56%)
Julia Burgen, District 5   1,260 (100%)
Pat Remington, District 8   5,967 (100%)

MAY 6, 2000
Sheri Capehart, District 2   1,218 (58.45%)

MAY 20, 2000 Runoff
Joe Bruner, winner, District 1   1,346 (59.88%)
    (Defeated Incumbent Nash)
Steve McCollum, winner, District 6   5,721 (69.87%)
Ron Wright, winner, District 7   5,001 (59.74%)

(Courtesy of City Secretary's Office, Arlington, Texas)

Appendix H

Arlington City Attorneys

Robert M. Burnett	January 1, 1962—February 28, 1965
Stanley Wilkes, Jr.	March 15, 1965—August 31, 1974
Tom Todd	January 10, 1975—May 31, 1986
Jay B. Doegey	March 17, 1986—

(Courtesy of City Secretary's Office, Arlington, Texas)

Notes

Chapter One
1. O.K. Carter (editorial writer and editorial page editor of the *Arlington Star-Telegram* and longtime columnist with Arlington *Citizen-Journal*), interviewed by the author, 12 January 1996.
2. Linda Gayda Miller, "Arlington's Population Growth from 1950 to 1955 and the Effects Refunding Contracts Had on Future Economic Growth" (The University of Texas at Arlington, History Department, unpublished research paper, Summer 1998), 2. Miller's paper was based on a series of primary sources and interviews with early city managers including O.B. Odell, William J. Pitstick, and Albert W. Rollins.
3. Ibid.
4. City Secretary's Office, Arlington, Texas, List of major events and dates in Arlington's history, Photocopy of typed list, No title, undated.
5. Ken Groves (Arlington City Council, 1978–1981, 1982–1983, 1984–1990), interviewed by the author, 28 August 1982.
6. Jewell Fox (longtime civic and Democratic party activist in Tarrant County, Texas), interviewed by the author, 15 March 1988.
7. Ibid.
8. Carma Borth (Department of Human Resources, Arlington, Texas), interviewed by the author, 15 January 1997.
9. Christopher Lee, "Council to Look at Expansion of Mayor's Powers, Pay, Hiring-policy Amendments among City Charter Proposals," *Dallas Morning News*, 1 January 1997, 1, 28A.
10. Ibid.
11. Ibid.
12. Mayor and City Council Office, Arlington, Texas, "Boards and Commissions Policy Statement," September 1997, 1–3.

Chapter Two
1. Arlington's population, a year earlier in 1950, was officially 7,692, City Secretary's Office, Arlington, Texas, List of major events and dates in Arlington's history. Photocopy of typed list. No title, undated.

2. Les Blaser (editor, *Arlington Daily News* 1972–1976), interviewed by the author, 6 January 1997.
3. Ibid.
4. Ibid.
5. Ibid.
6. Ibid.
7. O.K. Carter (editorial writer and editorial page editor of the *Arlington Star-Telegram* and longtime columnist with *Arlington Citizen-Journal*), interviewed by the author, 24 January 2000.
8. George Hawkes (former owner and publisher of Arlington *Citizen-Journal*), interviewed by the author, 2 December 1995.
9. Ibid.

Chapter Three
1. O.K. Carter (editorial writer and editorial page editor of the *Arlington Star-Telegram* and longtime columnist with Arlington *Citizen-Journal*), interviewed by the author, 12 January 1996.
2. Tom J. Vandergriff (Mayor of Arlington, Texas, 1951–1977), interviewed by the author, 30 December 1996.
3. Ibid.
4. In 1990, the City of Arlington and the Chamber of Commerce formally signed an agreement outlining the chamber's role in economic development. The city would pay the chamber $200,000 for economic development services. This agreement, however, was not completely embraced by all council members at the time and resulted in some debate and controversy.
5. James "Big Daddy" Knapp (longtime Arlington political observer, resident, large landowner, and civic activist), interviewed by the author, 12 May 1980.
6. Ibid.
7. Vandergriff, interview.
8. O.K. Carter. Presentation to Arlington Historical Society, 30 May 2000.
9. Harold Lasswell and Daniel Lerner, The Comparative Study of Elites (Stanford, California: Stanford University Press, 1952), 7.
10. For an elaborate and comprehensive overview of American politics as viewed by elite theorists see *The Irony of Democracy*, 8th. edition by Thomas R. Dye and Harmon Ziegler (Pacific Grove, California: Brooks/Cole Publishers, 1990). In particular note page 135 of this edition.
11. Ibid, 367.
12. Carol Estes Thometz, *The Decision Makers: The Power Structure in Dallas* (Dallas: Southern Methodist University Press, 1963).
13. Dr. R.G. "Wick" Alexander (Arlington City Council, 1971–1977), interviewed by the author, 21 November 1995.
14. Linda Gayda Miller, "Arlington's Population Growth from 1950 to 1955 and the Effects Refunding Contracts Had on Future Economic

Growth" (The University of Texas at Arlington, History Department, unpublished research paper, Summer 1998), 6.

15. Ibid., 11–12.

16. Ibid., 9.

17. In writing this study the author found many media representatives in various parts of the state acquainted and knowledgeable about the mayoral tenure of Tom J. Vandergriff.

18. Under a city manager form of government neither the mayor nor the members of the council are to perform daily affairs of government. The mayor and council have policy-making responsibility and not one of detail. Daily duties are under the authority of the city manager and city administration.

19. Samuel Hamlett (Arlington City Council, 1977–1979), interviewed by the author, 10 February 1997.

20. Vandergriff, interview.

21. Bill Baker (Vice-President for Academic Affairs, University of Texas at Tyler and former Vice-President for Academic Affairs, The University of Texas at Arlington), interviewed by the author, 18 September 2000.

22. George Hawkes (longtime Arlington civic leader and publisher of the Arlington *Citizen-Journal* newspaper), 2 December 1995.

23. Ibid.

24. Hawkes, interview. Also, Howard Wilemon (longtime city banker and former Chairman of the Board of Arlington Bank and Trust), interviewed by the author, 10 February 1997.

25. Throughout the years there were name changes for both Arlington banks. Arlington State became Arlington Bank and Trust, and eventually was taken over by Texas Commerce Bank. First National Bank became First City Bank. It too was taken over by Texas Commerce. Texas Commerce eventually closed down First City Bank.

26. Tony Arangio (longtime civic activist and a member of Downtown Rotary from 1974–1990), interviewed by the author, 13 February 1997.

27. Dan Gould, Jr. (member of a prominent and longtime Arlington real estate family), interviewed by the author, 2 June 2000.

28. Maxine Roane (longtime political supporter and activist in Tom Vandergriff's many campaigns), interviewed by the author, 29 September 1995.

29. In 1989, Tom Vandergriff sold the Chevrolet dealership to his son, Victor Vandergriff, Richard Greene, and other investors. In 1997, Richard Greene and the other investors sold the dealership to a Kansas-based firm, VT Inc.

30. James Knapp had owned some of the land eventually developed into Great Southwest Development. James "Big Daddy" Knapp (longtime Arlington political observer, resident, large landowner, and civic activist), interviewed by the author, 12 May 1980.

31. Ibid.

32. Ginger Vandergriff Deering (longtime Arlington resident, sister of Tom Vandergriff), interviewed by the author, 5 February 1997.

Chapter Four

1. S.J. Stovall (Arlington City Council, 1973–1977, Mayor of Arlington, Texas, 1977–1983), interviewed by the author, 5 December 1995.

2. Dr. R.G. "Wick" Alexander (Arlington City Council, 1971-1977), interviewed by the author, 21 November 1995.

3. "Timeline Series," *Arlington Morning News*, 17 January 1997, 7A.

4. Alexander, interview.

5. Stovall, interview.

6. Ibid.

7. Dan Gould, Jr. (member of a prominent and longtime Arlington real estate family), interviewed by the author, 2 June 2000.

8. Les Blaser (editor, *Arlington Daily News* 1972-1976), interviewed by the author, 6 January 1997.

9. Betty Fischer and Nile Fischer (longstanding activists in and observers of Arlington city and Democratic Party politics), interviewed by the author, 4 June 1996.

10. Stovall, interview.

11. Ibid.

12. Previous to his terms as a Tarrant County Commissioner, Jerry Mebus had served as an Arlington City council member as well.

13. Harold Patterson (Arlington City Council, 1966-1983; Mayor of Arlington, Texas, 1983-1987), interviewed by the author, 2 January 1996.

14. Ibid.

15. Ibid.

16. Ibid.

17. Richard Greene (Arlington City Council, 1984-1987; Mayor, City of Arlington, Texas, 1987-1997), interviewed by the author, 21 June 1996.

18. Dottie Lynn (Arlington City Council, 1982-2000), interviewed by the author, 26 January 1996.

19. "Timeline Series," *Arlington Morning News*, 17 January 1997, 7A.

20. Lynn, interview.

Chapter Five

1. Betty Fischer and Nile Fischer (longstanding activists in and observers of Arlington city and Democratic Party politics), interviewed by the author, 4 June 1996.

2. Ken Groves (Arlington City Council, 1978-1981,1982-1983,1984-1990), interviewed by the author, 5 April 1986.

3. Betty and Nile Fischer, interview.

4. Ibid.

5. The first election under a modified single member district system was in 1994. Now, council posts would be specified as "districts."

6. Betty and Nile Fischer, interview.

7. Barton Thompson (Arlington City Council, 1970-1972), interviewed by the author, 19 October 1995.

8. The plan to construct the convention center and also enter into a financial arrangement with a hotel on sections of the land was very controversial when proposed. The city proposed it as a way to alleviate some of the incurred debt and put the old Seven Seas land to use.

9. Martha Walker (Arlington City Council, 1972–1982), interviewed by the author, 12 October 1995.

10. Ibid.

11. Ibid.

12. Ibid.

13. Ibid.

14. James Cribbs (longtime resident, attorney in private practice, civic activist, and Republican Party leader), interviewed by the author, 1 March 1996.

15. Conversation with Paul Yarbrough, the same day as the Saxe-Snider run-off election, 6 May 1975.

16. Groves interview, 1 May 1988.

17. Ralph Shelton (Arlington City Council, 1972–1976), interviewed by the author, 27 October 1995.

18. Ibid.

19. Ibid

20. Cribbs, interview.

21. Ibid. Also, George Hawkes (longtime Arlington civic leader and publisher of the Arlington *Citizen-Journal* newspaper), 2 December 1995.

22. Samuel Hamlett (Arlington City Council, 1977–1979), interviewed by the author, 10 February 1997.

23. Jeanette Groves Proctor (widow of Ken Groves, former council member), interviewed by the author, 20 March 1996.

24. Penny Patrick (Executive Director, Theatre Arlington), interviewed by the author, 9 June 2000.

25. Jim Norwood (Arlington City Council, 1984–1986), interviewed by the author, 18 December 1996.

26. Dick Malec (Arlington City Council, 1986–1992), interviewed by the author, 12 February 1997.

27. Ibid.

28. Hawkes, interview.

29. Ibid.

30. Ibid.

31. The Dallas Fort Worth Turnpike opened in 1956 and later became Interstate 30 after the turnpike bonds were retired.

32. Hawkes, interview.

33. Ibid.

34. Ibid.

35. Cribbs, interview.

36. Hawkes, interview.

37. Ibid.

38. Dr. R.G. "Wick" Alexander (Arlington City Council, 1971–1977), interviewed by the author, 21 November 1995.

39. Ibid.

40. Ibid.

41. Ibid.

42. James Martin (Superintendent of Arlington Independent School District, 1955–1976), interviewed by the author, 6 January 1996.

43. Ibid.

44. Dottie Lynn (Arlington City Council, 1982–2000), interviewed by the author, 26 January 1996.

45. Ibid.

46. Kelly Jones (Arlington City Council, 1985–1989), interviewed by the author, 7 January 1998.

47. Ibid.

48. Ibid.

49. Roger "Rocky" Walton (Arlington City Council, 1990–1994), interviewed by the author, 4 January 1998.

50. Ibid.

51. Kay Taebel (Arlington City Council, 1993–1995), interviewed by the author, 25 November 1995.

52. See vote results of single member district election, table 1.1

53. Taebel, interview.

54. Ibid.

55. Ibid.

56. Ibid.

57. Groves, interview, 4 April 1986.

58. Miller, "Arlington's Population Growth from 1950 to 1955 and the Effects Refunding Contracts had on Future Economic Growth," 5.

59. City Secretary's Office, Arlington, Texas. List of major events and dates in Arlington's history. Photocopy of typed list. No title, undated.

60. Miller, "Arlington's Population Growth from 1950 to 1955 and the Effects Refunding Contracts had on Future Economic Growth," 6.

61. Ibid., 7.

62. Ross Calhoun (City Manager of Arlington, Texas, 1973–1984), interviewed by the author, 15 June 1996.

63. The entertainment park opened in 1972 as Seven Seas and was operated under that name by the city until the fall, 1974. Then the city tried leasing the park out under a different theme using the name Hawaii Kai. The entire theme park was permanently closed in 1975.

64. Calhoun, interview.

65. Ibid.

66. Ibid.

67. Ibid.

68. Jones, interview.

69. Walker, interview.

70. William Kirchoff (City Manager of Arlington, Texas, 1984–1991), interviewed by the author, 17 December 1996.
71. Ibid.
72. Ibid
73. Jones, interview.
74. Kirchoff, interview.
75. Ibid.
76. Ibid.
77. Elzie Odom (Arlington City Council, 1990–1997, Mayor of Arlington, 1997–), interviewed by the author, 29 December 1997.
78. Ibid.

Chapter Six
1. Joyce Morgan (former president, Arlington Chapter, League of Women Voters), interviewed by the author, 5 July 1996.
2. Ibid.
3. Ibid.
4. Lico Reyes (political and civic activist, city council candidate), interviewed by the author, 7 February 1997.
5. Ibid.
6. Roy George "Skippy" Brown III (civic activist, council candidate), interviewed by the author, 11 February 1997.
7. Among the major developments that early on drew her concern and attention were the St. Andrews Addition and the Baird Farm Development.
8. Kathy Howe (civic activist, homeowner advocate, and council candidate in 1985), interviewed by the author, 23 January 1997.
9. Jim Runzheimer (civic activist, attorney), interviewed by the author, 8 June 2000.

Index

A

adult video ordinance, 97
Albee, Edward, 96
Alexander, Dr. R.G. "Wick," 7, 42, 44, 46, 104-107
Altman, W.F., 16, 101
Anaheim, California, 23
Angus Wynne Freeway, 41
Animal Shelter Advisory Committee, 13
Appleton, "Roasty," 32
Arlington Bank and Trust, 103
Arlington Bar Association, 81
Arlington Board of Realtors, 36, 87
Arlington Boys and Girls Club, 136
Arlington Chamber of Commerce, 23-24, 34, 36, 120, 116
Arlington Citizen, 16, 101
Arlington Citizen-Journal, 16, 18, 36, 37, 76, 81, 101, 135, 146
Arlington City Hall, 20
Arlington City Commissioners, 5
Arlington Community Center, 78
Arlington Convention Center, 47, 84
Arlington Daily News, 16, 18, 47, 85
Arlington Downs, 2, 24
Arlington High School, 31, 108
Arlington Human Service Planners, 104
Arlington Independent School District, 81, 105, 107-109, 117, 119
Arlington Jaycees, 50, 74, 76
Arlington Journal, 16, 101

Arlington Memorial Hospital, 21, 41
Arlington Morning News, 18, 146
Arlington Museum of Art, 143
Arlington National Bank, 55
Arlington News-Texan, 16
Arlington Rotary Club, 33, 36
Arlington Savings, 59-60
Arlington School Board, 105, 117, 119
Arlington Stadium, 124
Arlington Star-Telegram, 1, 60
Arlington State Bank, 19, 35, 36, 59, 81, 103
Arlington State College, 2, 16, 30, 31, 33, 36, 42, 82, 89, 101
Arlington, Texas: airport in, 15; animal control/shelter in, 106, 126; and annexation, 52, 82-83, 123, 146; appointments to city office in, 10, 13, 14; beautification of, 115-116; boards and commissions of, 12-14, 42, 61, 91, 95, 130-131; bond issues in, 37, 52, 65, 73, 103, 109, 115, 124-125; bond rating of, 47, 58, 91; budget of, 68, 129; businesses in, 2, 22, 28, 39, 41-42, 55, 61, 65-66, 68, 69, 96-98; city attorney of, 10; City Council of, 4, 6, 10-11, 13, 14, 32, 34, 42-43, 50, 52, 55, 61-63, 69, 74, 76-79, 80-88, 96, 105-107, 109-112, 114, 118-119, 121, 127, 129, 130; city manager of, 4, 10, 29-30, 99, 102, 122-129; civic clubs in, 36-37; city charter of, 4, 6-7; commercial districts of, 23;

181

commission form of government in, 3-4; commissioners, 3 (*also see* City Council); convention center, 125-126; council-manager form of government in, 4, 10, 11, 12, 99, 122, 127; downtown area of, 23; essential services in 11, 28, 65, 73, 92, 102, 123; horseracing in, 2; incorporated, 1; land area of, 1, 15, 23, 35-36, 41, 69, 82-83, 145; library in, 104, 106, 115; liquor sales in, 103-104; mass transit in, 133-134; mayoral pay in, 6; mayoral term in, 3; mayoral veto in, 10; mayoral votes in, 6, 9; minorities in, 130; municipal judge of, 10; named, 1; nonpartisanship in, 9; ordinances of 11, 116, 119; place system in, 74; population of, 1, 4, 6, 15, 22, 29, 69, 101, 122; public housing in, 126; schools in, 107-109; social makeup of, 19; strong-mayor form of government in, 12; taxes in, 52, 65, 66-68, 69, 74-76, 79-80, 87, 90, 109, 110, 143; tourism in, 41-42, 47-48; water sources for, 15, 40-41, 55, 73, 106; weak-mayor form of government in, 10, 119; and zoning issues, 10, 52, 84-85, 111, 140-142, 145 (*also see* Planning and Zoning Commission)
Armey, Dick, 54, 66
Ashworth, Clyde, 103

B

Baird Farm, 52
Ball, John, 42, 76, 81
Ballpark, 21, 143
Barksdale, E.C., 33, 89
Barksdale, Marge, 33, 89
Barnes, B.C. "Barney," 15-16, 17, 24, 25, 101
Barney, Jen, 112
Bartlett, Steve, 12
Bell Helicopter, 110
Belo Corporation, 16, 18, 146
Bennet, Bill, 7

Bentham, Jeremy, 93
Berman, Leo, 34, 81-92, 112
Bielinski, Leo, 142
Big Brothers, 104
Blaser, Les, 16-18, 47
Blumberg, Dr. Elliot, 61
Boles, Truett, 117
Bondurant, Rick, 118
Bowen Road, 83
Brashear, Donna, 128
Briscoe, Dolph, 82
Brooklyn Dodgers, 32
Brooks, Theron, 129, 130
Brown, Charles, 42, 52
Brown, Roy George "Skippy," III, 137-139
Bruner, Gary, 56-58
Buchanan, M.D. "Buck," 55

C

Calhoun, Ross, 123, 124, 125, 126-127
campaigns, 37, 61-65, 74, 76-77, 78-82, 84, 107, 114
Campbell, George, 127, 129
Capital Cities Corporation, 146
Carlisle Military Academy, 119
Carrollton, Texas, 22
Carter, O.K., 1
CATO Institute, 129
Chicago, Illinois, 12
Church Women United, 64, 82
Cibola Inn, 52
civil service system, 10
Coble, Wayne, 49. 120
Collins, Benton, 102
Concerned Taypayers of Arlington, 143
conflict of interest, 9
Connally, John, 33
convenience stores, 98
Cooper Street, 93-95
Corps of Engineers, 42
Cotton Bowl, 66
council-manager form of government, 4, 10, 11, 12, 99, 122, 127
Cravens, Carlisle, 19, 36, 119, 121-122

Index

Cravens, Tom, 6-7, 88, 108, 119-122
Cravens family, 19, 36
Cravens Park, 122
Cribbs, James, 86, 87, 88, 90
Cribbs, Ott, 86
Cribbs law firm, 86
Crippen, Jack, 50, 73

D

Daley, Richard, 129
Dallas Citizen's Council, 27, 46
Dallas Cowboys, 66
Dallas Morning News, 17, 18, 85, 98
Dallas, Texas, 4, 11-12, 27, 66, 147
Dallas-Fort Worth Turnpike, 39-40, 41, 103
Day, Darrell, 138
Decision Analyst, 2
Deering, Ginger Vandergriff, 41
Dipert, Dan, 117
Disney Corporation, 146
Division, 106
Doskocil Manufacturing, 2, 68
Dottie Lynn Recreation Center, 112
Downtown Rotary, 108
Downtown Rotary Club, 36-37, 102, 108
Dunsworth, H.A.D., 34, 42, 50
Dye, Thomas, 26

E

East, Rev. Henard, 50
Eastland, Bill, 139, 140
Eastland, Terry, 139
El Paso, Texas, 27
elitist theory of government, 26-28, 32, 36, 80-81, 85, 88, 91, 120, 145, 147
English, Roy, 115
Eppstein, Bryan, 65, 114
Estes, Ralph, 74
Ewen, Joe, 116, 130

F

"Facts and Issues," 133
"Familes in Crisis," 98
Farenthold, Frances "Sissy," 82

Farrar, Billie, 106, 107
Federalist Papers, 93
Fielder Road, 106
financial disclosure, 7
First Baptist Church (Arlington), 48, 101, 105, 108, 113
First National Bank (Arlington), 19, 35, 36, 103
First National Bank (Grand Prairie), 35
First United Methodist Church (Arlington), 36, 105, 108, 113
Fischer, Betty, 61, 71, 88, 90, 105, 110, 142
Fischer, Nile, 61, 71, 88, 90
Fort Worth Star-Telegram, 18, 85, 146
Fort Worth, Texas, 12, 27, 82-83, 98, 121-122, 147
Fox, Jewell, 9
Frost, Martin, 65, 72

G

General Motors, 2, 22, 24, 25, 28, 32, 40, 65, 68, 69
Gladden, Don, 71
Good Government League, 27
Gould, Dan, Jr., 47
Grand Prairie, 15, 24, 35, 40, 88, 103
Grand Prairie State, 35
Great Southwest Corporation, 84, 123-124
Great Southwest Development, 39
Great Southwest Industrial District, 41
Green Oaks Boulevard, 68, 111, 112
Greene, Richard, 3, 14, 39, 42, 43, 58-70, 79, 92, 93, 110, 112, 114, 119, 128, 139, 145
Groves, Ken, 50, 52, 53, 61, 62, 65, 73, 79, 91, 92-95, 107, 108, 112, 129, 130, 135

H

Hamlett, Sam, 34, 74, 79, 88-92
Hampton, Lynn, 128
Harris, Grady, 138

Hawaii Kai, 84, 124
Hawkes, George, 16, 18, 35, 81, 88, 101-104, 107, 108
Henz, Bernadette, 7
Hightower, Paula, 130
Highway 303, 40
Highway 360, 41
"Hill, The," 19
Holman, Dixon, 100
Hospital Authority, 13
Housing Authority Board, 13
Houston, Texas, 27
Howe, Kathy, 140-142
Hughes Corporation, 68
Hughes, Martha, 81
Huntley and Brinkley, 23
Huntley, Chet, 23

I

Interstate 20, 40
Interstate 30, 39
Irving, Texas, 22, 66

J

Jacobsen, Rose, 128
Jaggers, Jerry, 74, 76
Jenkins, Mike, 48
Johnson Creek, 93
Johnson, Lyndon Baines, 89
Jones, Albert, 4, 122
Jones, Kelly, 112-114

K

Kallam, Sally, 46
"Kelly Girls," 92
Kennard, Don, 72
Kennard, Jake, 112
Kennedale Church Oak Crest Baptist Church, 98
Kirchoff, William E. "Bill," 99, 112, 114, 123, 127-129, 133
Kirmser, Kent, 118
Kiwanis Club, 33
Knapp, James "Big Daddy," 39, 40, 81, 88
Knight-Ridder Corporation, 146
Ku Klux Klan, 1-2
Kunkle, David, 127-128

L

Lake Arlington, 15, 41
Lasswell, Harold, 26
Leach, Dan, 56
Leadership Arlington, 46, 104
Leadership Fort Worth, 46
League of Women Voters, 78, 133, 134
Leatherman, Louise "Susie," 31-32
Lee, Robert E., 1
Library Board, 13
Lincoln, Abraham, 26
Locke, John, 93
Lone Star Gas, 122
LTV (Ling Temco Vought Corporation), 50, 73
Luttrell, James, 88
Lynn, Dottie, 62-65, 69, 109-112, 114

M

Malec, Richard (Dick), 98, 99-100, 112, 115, 127, 129
Maner, Doland, 42, 78
Marcotte, Richard, 62
Martin, Duane, 74
Martin, Eleanor Grace, 107
Martin, James, 81, 105, 107-109
Martin Sprocket and Gear, 2
Mathes, Curtis, 84
Mauzy, Oscar, 74
McClendon, Bruce, 96
McDavid Acura, 60
McFadin, Bill, 112
McFarland, Bob, 114
Meadowbrook Park, 28
Mebus, Jerry, 54
Merrill, Charles, 81
Mill, John Stuart, 93
Miller Business Systems, 2
Miller, Lynda Gayda, 29
Morgan, Joyce, 133-134
Mount Olive Baptist Church, 93, 130
Musgrove, Bob, 143

N

National Semiconductor, 2, 68

Index

NBC, 23
New York City, 12
North American Aviation, 103
North Texas Agricultural College, 101, 122
North Texas Higher Education Authority, 13
Northwestern University, 23
Norwood, Jim, 95-99

O

Odell, O.B., 4, 122-123
Odom, Elzie, 95, 129-131
Oil States Rubber, 2
Olympics, 60
Open Meetings Act, 3, 9, 52, 83, 85, 117, 146
Open Records Act, 3, 9, 116-117, 146
Optimist Club, 33
Orange, Texas, 129

P

Park Row, 106
Parks and Recreation Board, 13
Parties Portable, 135
partisan politics, 9
paternalistic form of government, 20
Patterson, Harold, 42, 49, 55-58, 60, 62, 64, 84, 108, 112, 126, 128
Pennsylvania Railroad, 84, 124
People for Accountable Government, 118
Peveto Bill, 79
Pikulinski, Jerry, 55
Pioneer Parkway, 40
Planning and Zoning Board/Commission, 13, 14, 42, 61, 63, 79, 81, 104, 106, 109, 111, 112, 114, 115, 130, 133, 142
Pope, Dr. Eugene, 108
Preiss, Elwood, 46
prohibition, 103-104
Purvis, Dixon, 42, 50

R

Rainey, Homer, 89
Randol Mill Park, 28, 96

Redondo Beach, California, 129
refunding contracts, 28-29
Rendon, 81
Reyes, Lico, 135-137
Richards, Ann, 66
Roane, Maxine, 38
Robinson, Harry, 91, 93, 134-135, 137, 139
Robinson, Reverend N.L., 93
Rollins, Al, 103
Rosentraub, Marc, 34
Rotary Club, 33, 36, 102, 108
run-off election, 6
Runzheimer, Jim, 143-144
Rupay, Judy, 115

S

Saint Maria Goretti Catholic Church, 82
San Antonio, Texas, 27
San Diego Sea Life, 84, 124
Sarducci, Guido, 136
Savings Banc, 60
Saxe, Allan, 7, 77, 78, 129
Schadt, Graham, 110
Serna, Dan, 119, 130
Seven Seas theme park, 16-18, 47, 84, 85-86, 110, 123-124, 125
Seventh Street Gang, 27
Shelton, Ralph, 81, 86-88
Sheraton Hotel, 125
Short, Bob, 22
single-member districts, 7, 8, 50-52, 79, 91, 117-118, 119, 146
Six Flags Over Texas, 2, 39, 41
"Skippy's Mistake," 137
smoking ordinances, 116, 119
Snider, Bill, 78
Snider, Carolyn, 37, 49, 78, 77-79, 110
Snider, Dr. Richard, 77
Southern Industrial Steel Company, 42, 78
State Board of Education, 119
State Republican Executive Committee, 86
Stephen F. Austin College, 114
Stovall, Mrs., 44

Stovall, S.J., 9, 42, 44, 46, 47-55, 60, 64, 84, 107, 108, 112, 126
Strickland, Bill, 126
strong-mayor form of government, 12
Sunbelt Savings, 60
Sutton, Willard, 42, 86

T

Taebel, Del, 34. 117
Taebel, Kay, 61, 117-119, 142
Tarrant Appraisal District, 80
Tarrant County, 81
Tarrant County Commissioners Court, 41, 54, 95, 115, 142
Tarrant County Democratic Party, 71
Tarrant County Jail, 98
telephone banks, 37, 38
Texas A&M System, 33
Texas College of Osteopathic Medicine, 120-122
Texas Electric, 122
Texas Property Tax Code, 79
Texas Rangers, 2, 18, 21, 22, 66-68, 69, 120
Theatre Arlington, 95-96
Thometz, Carol Estes, 27
Thompson, Barton, 81-82, 83-84, 108
Thompson, Clarence, 81
Thornton, Z. Joe, 85
Todd, Tom, 49
"town versus gown," 33
Town North Shopping Center, 15
Turner, Dee, 142
Turnpike Stadium, 124

U

United Way Campaign, 104
University of North Texas, 122
University of Southern California, 23
University of Texas at Austin, 120
University of Texas at Arlington, 16, 31, 33-35, 87, 94, 95, 101, 119, 117-118
University of Texas System, 33

Upchurch, Lon, 143

V

Van Ravenswaay, Marti, 142
Vandergriff Acura, 60
Vandergriff Park, 21, 39
Vandergriff Pavilion, 21
Vandergriff, Tom, 6, 14, 17, 18, 20-43, 44-51, 52, 54, 55, 58, 60, 61, 64, 66, 69, 70, 71, 80, 82, 86, 87, 88, 95, 101, 104, 107, 109, 112, 122, 123, 126, 145
Vandergriff, W.T. "Hooker," 19, 22, 25, 36, 119, 120, 121-122
Veselka, Herman, 7
voter registration, 78
voter turnout, 27, 50, 66
Voters Organized for Community Awareness and Leadership (VOCAL), 142
voting: at-large, 7; electronic, 6; single district, 7, 8, 50-52, 79, 91, 117-118, 119, 146

W

Walker, Martha, 82, 83, 84, 109, 110, 127, 131
Wallace, Frank, 50
Walther, Larry, 34, 98
Walton, Roger "Rocky," 99, 115-117
Washington Senators, 22, 120
water fluoridation, 55, 73
Watson, O.L., 54
weak-mayor from of government, 10, 119
Weatherford, Texas, 25
Wells, Max, 12
WFAA-TV, 51
Wharton, Paul, 48
Wicker, Christine, 85
Wilemon, Claude, 36
Wilemon, Howard, 19, 36, 59, 81, 112
Wilemon family, 19, 36
Willis, Ted, 116
Wimbledon Homeowner's Association, 115
Wolfe, Don, 91

Index

Woodland West, 112
Wright, Jim, 25, 89
Wynne, Angus, 39, 41

Y

Yarborough, Ralph, 72
Yarbrough, Paul, 81, 85-88, 90
YMCA, 104

Young Men for Arlington, 50, 76, 87
Youth and Families Board, 13

Z

Zeckendorf, Bill, 39
Zeigler, Harmon, 26
Zoning Board of Adjustment, 13, 87

www.ingramcontent.com/pod-product-compliance
Lightning Source LLC
Chambersburg PA
CBHW050552160426
43199CB00015B/2630